fREEiNG
THE.
GENiE
within

## About the Author

Debra Lynne Katz is the author of the groundbreaking work *You Are Psychic: The Art of Clairvoyant Reading & Healing*. An internationally acclaimed clairvoyant reader, healer, teacher, and spiritual counselor, Debra is the founder of the International School of Clairvoyance. She holds a bachelor's degree in psychology and a master's degree in social work, and is a former federal probation officer. Debra has studied at the top psychic training schools in the United States and with a variety of faith healers in the Philippines. She was the host of *The Psychic Explorer*, a popular television show in Sedona, Arizona. Her second book is *Extraordinary Psychic: Proven Techniques to Master Your Natural Psychic Abilities*. An aspiring director and screenwriter, Debra lives in Moorpark, California. Please visit her website at www.urpsychic.com, where you will also find her contact information.

Debra Lynne Katz

# fREEiNG
## THE
# GENIE
## within

Manifesting Abundance,
Creativity & Success in Your Life

Llewellyn Publications
Woodbury, Minnesota

First Edition
Second Printing, 2009

Book design by Steffani Sawyer
Cover art © 2009 Nguyen Tuan Khang
Cover design by Ellen Dahl
Editing by Brett Fechheimer

Llewellyn is a registered trademark of Llewellyn Worldwide, Ltd.

Excerpts from *Life and Teaching of the Masters of the Far East*, by Baird T. Spalding, are reprinted with permission of DeVorss & Company.

**Library of Congress Cataloging-in-Publication Data**
Katz, Debra Lynne, 1968–
  Freeing the genie within : manifesting abundance, creativity & success in your life / by Debra Lynne Katz. — 1st ed.
      p.  cm.
  Includes bibliographical references.
  ISBN 978-0-7387-1475-2
  1.  Self-actualization (Psychology)—Miscellanea. 2.  Success—Psychic aspects. 3.  Katz, Debra Lynne, 1968– I. Title.
  BF1045.S44.K38 2009
  131—dc22
                                      2009000749

Llewellyn Worldwide does not participate in, endorse, or have any authority or responsibility concerning private business transactions between our authors and the public.
  All mail addressed to the author is forwarded but the publisher cannot, unless specifically instructed by the author, give out an address · or phone number.
  Any Internet references contained in this work are current at publication time, but the publisher cannot guarantee that a specific location will continue to be maintained. Please refer to the publisher's website for links to authors' websites and other sources.

Llewellyn Publications
A Division of Llewellyn Worldwide, Ltd.
2143 Woodbury Drive, Dept. 978-07387-1475-2
Woodbury, Minnesota 55125-2989, U.S.A.
www.llewellyn.com

Printed in the United States of America

## Acknowledgments

Many thanks to Carrie Obry, my acquisitions editor at Llewellyn, who encouraged me to write this book, as well as to my production editor, Brett Fechheimer, who wasn't scared away by my last one. Thank you to my dear friends and teaching partners, Francine Marie Sheppard and Kazandrah Martin, who I swear are getting younger each year. Thanks to Rachel Mai, who manifested a house on a ranch nestled up beside a haystack after filling up her manifestation box with hay. I look forward to discovering what else emerges from that box! Thank you also to Christie Thompson, Darrah Waters, Tony Carito, and to the members of my writing group—Melanie Smith, Gary Weinberg, Lyena Strelkoff, Dean Purvis, and James C. Cremin. A special thanks to Amanda Robinson, who helped make my short film *Bending Spoons* (now on YouTube) possible, and who helped me get back in touch with my creativity. Thanks to my psychic twin sister, Amy Beth Katz, to Eric Lauderdale, brother Brad Katz, and sister-in-law Rachel Katz, for helping out with Manny this past year and editing my film. Thanks to my parents, Nedra Katz and Robert Katz, and their spouses, Dale and Dottie, for looking after Manny when I have not been available. Much gratitude to my current teachers, Michael and Raphaelle Tamura. Thank you to my clairvoyant students and clients, who reminded me this past year how much I really love my work. My life and this book would of course not be what they are without the teachings and support I was given so many years ago by my clairvoyant teachers from northern California. Thanks again to my son and soul mate, Manny Felipe Katz, and to my sweetie, Danny Kohler, for giving me all that time and space to write, and for doing all those loads of laundry!

# CONTENTS

To Manny and Danny

"My heart is afraid that it will have to suffer,"
the boy told the alchemist . . .
"Tell your heart that the fear of suffering is worse
than the suffering itself . . . "
"Every second of the search is an encounter with God,"
the boy told his heart.
"When I have been truly searching for my treasure,
every day has been luminous,
because I've known that every hour was a part
of the dream that I would find it . . .
I've discovered things along the way
that I never would have seen had I not
had the courage to try things that seemed impossible
for a shepherd to achieve . . . "
That night, the boy slept deeply, and, when he awoke,
his heart began to tell him things that came
from the Soul of the World.

— PAULO COELHO, *The Alchemist*

Travelers, it is late. Life's sun is going to set. During these brief days
that you have strength, be quick and spare no effort of your wings.
—Rumi

# I

# INTRODUCTION

About nine years ago I was working as a clairvoyant
reader at a New Age bookstore in Sedona, Arizona.
I had just paid my rent and I was completely broke.
It was past lunchtime, and I was hungry and well on
my way to feeling sorry for myself. Then I remem-
bered that I actually did possess all the knowledge I
needed to manifest something as simple as lunch, so I
decided I was going to do a little experiment. I closed
the door to my office, sat down in my favorite chair,
and declared that I was not going to get up until I had

manifested something to eat. Not just anything but something I really loved, like Chinese food.

Next came the doubts. How long might I really have to sit here? What would the baby sitter say if I told her I wasn't going to be able to pick up Manny until next week? But I pushed aside these pesky thoughts and got busy. First, in order to psych myself up for success, I reminded myself of all the things I had created over the last couple of decades. These included trips and cars, furniture and spiritual teachers, friends, jobs, and more peace and joy than I had ever thought possible in my younger years. Next, I conjured up a feeling of gratitude for where I was in the present moment. I reminded myself that I wouldn't be sitting here in this room, doing the work I loved, in one of the most stunning and mystical places on earth if it wasn't for my ability to create what I needed, when I really needed it. Now I was ready for the core technique: I visualized myself being handed a hearty plate of steaming food that tasted and smelled so good that it tumbled from my lips because my smile was so big.

I had barely settled into my meditation when there was a knock at my door. It was Scottie, whose office was down the hall. She was a busy woman who rarely had time to chat with a newcomer like myself.

"Hey, you've probably already eaten, but I was just wondering if you might like to join me for lunch as my guest," Scottie said.

Hmmm, that was a hard one!

"There's only one catch," she warned. "I'm really craving some Chinese food. Is that okay with you?"

When I arrived back at my office after this fulfilling lunch, I found a box of warm cookies outside my door that a client had baked for me. A few minutes later, a man came to see me for a reading. He was a famous radio sports announcer. After our session, he invited me to join him for dinner at L'Auberge, the only French restaurant in Sedona—and part of a very expensive resort. Before that night, the only time I had ever set foot in their plush lobby was when I'd applied for a job, for which I'd been turned down (which was fine with me; I'm no waitress). That night we had a fantastic dinner, despite the fact that he showed up in a bright yellow pinstriped suit. I can't recall what I ate—heck, I probably couldn't even pronounce it—but I sure remember the champagne! The bill came to over two hundred and fifty dollars, but the sports announcer refused to let me pay a penny, which was good—because I still didn't have a penny.

That's what an inner genie will do for you when you remember to release her from her bottle.

### Embracing the genie within

There is a force within each of us as powerful as creation itself. Perhaps it *is* creation itself. It is that which manifested our bodies and all that we experience here on this crazy place we call Earth. This creative force has the ability to draw to us whatever we really, truly need and desire. Some people may call this force God, but I like to call it the *genie within*. Like the genie of countless stories, it is bottled up inside, waiting to serve us with undying devotion. When our genies are awakened from their slumber, there is nothing they won't and can't do for us. Our genies are our servants and our creative muses. Like Peter Pan's Tinker Bell (okay, she was a fairy, but never mind), the more we believe in them, the stronger their powers grow.

Conversely, the more we ignore our genies, the dimmer their light becomes—until we lose all sense of them. This is when we feel disconnected, alone, hopeless, and broken. The good news is that our genies never truly leave us. They are always working hard on our behalf around the clock; it's just that they require strong leadership. The clearer the directives we give our genies, the better the results. The question of course is: how can we give them clear directives when we ourselves are not always clear? After working with hundreds of self-proclaimed "confused" people, I could write a whole book about that challenge—in fact, you are reading it now!

### The problem with wishing

If you think back to any story involving a genie, you will recall that there was always some limit to the wishes the genie was willing or able to grant. Either the wishes were restricted to three, or there were some unfavorable stipulations attached. The protagonist—perhaps a wannabe prince, a clumsy knight, or a battered fisherman—just about always messed up this opportunity of a lifetime by wishing for something much smaller and less helpful to him than *we* as observers would have chosen for him—or for ourselves. Other times he was indeed granted his wish but instead of it bringing him happiness, it only served to complicate things.

One of the most frustrating things about these stories is that the wisher rarely just wishes for an unlimited stockpile of wishes, which is certainly what you or I would have done if we were lucky enough to be in his shoes, right? Hmmm . . . maybe, maybe not. Did it ever occur to you that you might actually *be* in his shoes right now? Not just in terms of your wishing power, but in the way your own wishes may be misguided or limited?

An interesting thing about these fairy-tale protagonists is that they are always the underdog. They seem to have lots of wishes, but not a whole lot of power, self-confidence, or focused concentration. I suspect that if instead of making three wishes, they had made three *intentions*, three *determinations*, or three *proclamations*, they would have fared better. After all, these words project a much greater sense of strength than the word *wish*, which holds an inherent feeling of ungrounded dreaminess, of longing and waiting and hoping. I wonder, have you been doing more wishing or more proclaiming lately? Beggars beg, fairy-tale prince wannabes wish, but kings, queens, and presidents proclaim!

Of course for some of the unlikely heroes in our favorite stories, whether fictional or our own, it isn't so much about what is being wished for or how the wish is being wished, but rather whether the wisher/ dreamer/ hoper feels worthy of receiving the wish. Perhaps in these all-too-familiar tales, it isn't the genie that needs to be freed from the tiny bottle, but rather the one who wishes.

**What to wish for?**
Whether you are seeking greater peace, love, or all the riches in the world, I believe it boils down to this: if you would like to be king or queen, is wishing for the jeweled crown or the fancy title really the wisest wish? A servant who is handed a crown will never be a king, or remain one for very long, if he doesn't transform his *identity* from servant to king. This means he must not only believe himself already to be a king, but he must also really know how to carry out the duties and responsibilities of a king in a king-like fashion.

This doesn't rule out the possibility that he might end up king—or, for that matter, president of the United States—before he is ready. He may be given fancy clothes and a nice bed to sleep in—and perhaps even some nice young ladies to sleep with (which may be more than enough for some!)—but he will quickly be deposed by his people, his adversaries, and even his closest advisors (perhaps including those young ladies), who may be more king- or queen-like than he is. Wouldn't that servant better serve himself with a wish—no, scratch that, with a *proclamation*—that he will soon manifest in himself king-like qualities that others will subsequently recognize and reward?

Such a process may, of course, take more time than he—or you—were hoping for. But the cool thing is that in the end you will enjoy your new and improved identity whether or not you really do end up with that official title (perhaps by then you won't even want or need it). And if you do end up in a castle or the White House, you will be able to spend your time enjoying your reign from your throne, as opposed to wallowing in the moat because the job was way too much for you and your little star-studded crown to handle.

## The problem with butterflies

I have a love-hate relationship with butterflies. Their transformation from a rather drab, slow, wormlike thing to a brilliant, colorful being that can fly elevates them to a magical, even enviable, status to us humans who are still very much confined to the ground. They are a symbol of change, of hope, of the creative power brewing within the cocoons of our own hearts and souls that whispers promises of flight from what we are to what we long to become.

That's all fine; however, the problem is this: butterflies are insects and I, like many of you, don't like insects. There is always the chance one will land in our hair or spew a bunch of maggot eggs on our hamburger. There is always the danger we will swat it or accidentally smash it, and incur a karmic debt as its executioner. However, the main problem I have with butterflies is that they just make this whole transformation thing look so darn easy—at least to the casual observer who really doesn't get to see what's going on inside the silent, steady cocoon. Now if the cocoon swayed violently from side to side, emitting little butterfly screams rivaling the frightened clamoring of our minds when we're going through a similar period of growth, then we'd have something in common with these beady-eyed guys. But instead it appears as if they just weave themselves a cozy little sleeping bag, take a nice long siesta, and *voilà*—there they are in all their winged glory: no sweat, no tears, no three-hundred-dollar telephone or psychiatric bill. That's just not fair!

### Caterpillar soup

I am fortunate to belong to a spiritually oriented screenwriters group, of which Lyena Strelkoff is a member. Lyena is the creator and star of a one-woman show called *Caterpillar Soup*. Her story begins on the day she had the best and last orgasm of her life. On this day, after making love to her new boyfriend, she had the urge to go frolic in the forest. She was feeling playful and climbed to the top of a tree, never suspecting that the limb she sat on was rotten underneath. The limb cracked, tumbled to the ground, and took her with it. Like the limb, Lyena's back snapped in half, and in one instant out of the millions of instants of her life, she became paralyzed from the waist down.

Lyena, who had been a dancer and an extremely independent, self-reliant woman, recalls the initial pain and difficulty of not being able to walk, bathe, or even use the bathroom on her own. However, the inner turmoil she experienced was even more challenging than coping with her physical disabilities. Without warning, all the former notions of who she was, what she was capable of, and what made her a worthwhile human being were ripped away. The fall from the tree didn't just take away her legs—it stole her identity. She no longer knew how to think or feel about herself. To make matters worse, anyone who even looked at her was quick to place a label on her, from complete strangers to the medical personnel who couldn't understand why she did something as "silly" as climbing a tree.

Lyena refers to her life after the accident as "caterpillar soup." She knew she still had some pieces of her old self left, but they were stewing in a murky, unfamiliar substance that did not look or feel the same from one day to the next. However, over time, by staying aware, curious, and hopeful, her spirit began to sprout wings of creativity she never knew she had. She feels her life is now more exciting and fulfilling than ever before. Part of this is because her loving boyfriend became her devoted husband and her partner in every sense of the word. Where she cannot go in her chair, he carries her.

During one of our meetings, during which Lyena discussed her plans to turn her successful one-woman show into a film, she shared that when she was falling from the tree, she did not feel any fear. She loved that tree, and as the branch cracked beneath her, she recalls having the thought, "There is nothing I can do to stop falling. I am just going to be present and observe the feeling of flight through the air." She said she felt only curiosity and peace during the fall, which seemed much longer than it must have taken.

I suspect if the rest of us adopted Lyena's attitude as we find ourselves letting go of the limbs that can no longer support us, we might be able to achieve that state of grace she now enjoys. She feels she has traded her legs for wings.

### The choice

Recently there has been a lot of talk about spiritual alchemy, the power of the mind, and the law of attraction. The main tenet of these concepts is that we can manifest our desires through thought alone. I believe that is true for some people, but not for all. It is only true for those of you who are willing to enter into the hot and murky soup of uncertainty, and remain there long enough until it turns you into something far more complex and tastier than you were before. It is only true if you are willing to let go of parts of yourself that may not have really been you in the first place. Otherwise, you may be destined to remain a caterpillar.

Don't get me wrong: being a caterpillar is not necessarily a bad thing to be. You'll still have plenty of leaves to eat and other caterpillars to hang out with. It's just that you'll end up moving much more slowly through life, with less freedom and more frustration.

This is a choice. It is your choice.

Don't worry about losing. If it is right, it happens.
The main thing is not to hurry. Nothing good gets away.
—JOHN STEINBECK

ב

# AMENDMENTS TO THE LAW OF ATTRACTION

If you haven't already noticed, just about everyone is reading—or writing—a book about the law of attraction. I define the *law of attraction* simply as the force, or invisible power, by which a body (your body) draws anything to itself while resisting separation from that same thing.

The emerging popularity of this subject is very exciting because I believe it reflects the current state in the evolution of mass consciousness—that mold from which we sprang or out of which we crawled, and that we constantly reshape through our thoughts and actions. I use the word *mold* because on several occasions in my work with clients struggling with feelings of depression and frustration, I had a vision of a plaster mold. In my vision, I'd see the part of my client still merged with the mold, while another part had already broken free. The part that had broken free was aware that there was more to life—more possibilities, more joy—than the client had previously believed, but the client was having trouble moving forward due to the part still in bondage. When I looked to see what the mold was made of, it consisted of the rules and beliefs of the client's parents and grandparents and of religious and political leaders, sometimes going back for generations, that had set the parameters for who my client had permission to be. This put a cap on what my client could achieve.

If you are over the age of thirty, you've likely heard the expression "When they made him, they threw away the mold" one too many times. This expression means, of course, that the subject is unique and different from what came before or will come after. Perhaps this expression was so popular because up until the first half of the last century, more people did seem to closely resemble their forefathers in thought and behavior. The molds were recycled over and over, so the "apple never fell too far from the tree" and there were more "chips off the old block" than there were new blocks. These are expressions our parents and grandparents bantered about mercilessly, as if they were the witty poets who invented them. Meanwhile, we the recipients found these clichés to be as irritating as a needle ripping its way across a vinyl record—not suspecting that, like our favorite 45s, these expressions were about to become obsolete.

These expressions are far less common today not just because we got so sick of them, but also because we have been undergoing a process of individuation that is allowing us to move further from the tree, from the mold, and from the block, so we can truly wake up to who we all really are as opposed to who we were told we were supposed to be. This in no way means we love the people who raised us any less. It does mean that perhaps we listen to them, follow them, and expect from them a little less, because now we see them for who they are, as opposed to who we were supposed to *believe* they were. (Gasp! There, I said it!—and as of yet, no guillotine has chopped off my insubordinate head, although my pencil just broke!)

Many people think it's the part of the self that is still stuck in the mold or cocoon or the primordial soup that's in pain, but I believe that it's the part that's half-freed that is the one suffering. This is where a majority of us are today. The other part that's still there trapped inside the mold doesn't know that it's there; rather, it's comfortable or even hanging on for dear life to all those familiar folk inside who don't want to let us go either. So it's the half-emancipated part that is desperately searching for how to extract its remaining leg or arm or eyeball. This is the part of you that brought your body to this book and the part of me that wrote it. Welcome! I knew we'd meet sooner or later! Now let's see what we can do to emancipate ourselves *completely*. Hmmm, when I wrote the word *completely*, I felt some *butterflies* in my stomach! How about you?!

### Why I wrote this book

When I was nineteen years old, I visited a psychic for the first time, in Murphysboro, Illinois. She told me three things I've never forgotten. The first news flash was that someday I'd be doing readings like she did. Of course I thought this was complete hogwash, since I had no idea how to control any of my abilities and didn't even know it was possible to learn to do psychic readings. The second thing she told me was that sometimes when I arrived at a new place I would be overwhelmed by all the energy, so I should always first go to the bathroom and ground myself before attempting to talk to anyone. (So what if it looked like I had a bladder-control problem?!) Her third bit of wisdom was the most important. She told me that the one thing I needed to do more than anything in all of life was to get my little buns (well, they were little in those days) to the bookstore and buy Joseph Murphy's book *The Power of Your Subconscious Mind*.

I wondered at first if maybe this psychic was a relative of Joseph Murphy or was going to make a commission somehow. However, when I saw that the book actually cost a lot less than the multitude of others there, I purchased it, read it, and reread it three more times by the end of the next day. Thus began a journey that has infused the last twenty-two years of my life with an unrelenting passion for this subject. It actually only took me a few months of direct application of Murphy's techniques to become convinced that my thoughts, both conscious and unconscious, did in fact influence my reality. However, my newfound spiritual practice was at times riddled with frustration, as it was obvious that success was not always instant or imminent. Therefore, I began a quest early on in my adulthood to understand why is it that these concepts, particularly the law of attraction, seemed to work sometimes but not always, and for some people but not for others.

As the years progressed, I continued to utilize the playground of my own life, and later that of my clients and students, as a real-life laboratory to explore these questions, the answers to which I will share with you on the following pages.

### How this book differs from others like it
I, like many of you, am tickled pink that this subject has reached mainstream consciousness. Every time one person gains awareness of their potential, it increases

our own. As individuals living within a society, we are like woven threads of a fabric, the fabric being our reality that dictates what is possible. Every time we change a thread, the fabric itself is altered. If you change enough threads, what was once a tired, gray sheath becomes a blazing, color-filled flag, sparkling with possibility and hope.

Popular films and bestsellers like the The Secret could not be enjoying the astounding success they are today if the path had not been paved by countless other trailblazers, including Joseph Murphy, Wayne Dyer, Jerry and Esther Hicks, Sonia Choquette, Jane Roberts, and the early spiritualists such as Edgar Cayce, Madame Blavatsky, Baird T. Spalding, and Paramahansa Yogananda (founder of the Self-Realization Fellowship and author of *Autobiography of a Yogi*). Millions of eyeballs are popping open all around the world thanks to these visionaries. However, I do feel that now is the time to move beyond the basics and to delve into some areas that have been either overlooked altogether or underemphasized in the previous writings. Let me emphasize: this is in no way due to any weakness on the part of the above-mentioned authors whom I hold in the highest esteem. Rather, these works have led to an awakening of massive numbers of people who are now ready for new or updated information.

**Missing pieces of the alchemic puzzle**
**that will be addressed in this book**

*Aggravated alchemists*

*Spiritual alchemy* refers to the transformation of one form of matter or experience into another, by utilizing one's full range of spiritual abilities. Many folks on the path of conscious creating are seeing radical results in some areas of their lives, but are feeling stuck or unsuccessful in other particular areas. Like a physician or shaman who cannot cure someone, a psychic who draws a blank, or a teacher who doesn't have an answer, many spiritual alchemists, whether experienced practitioners or ordinary people who understand the basic concepts, are beating themselves up for not being good enough manifesters.

This feeling of not meeting their own unrealistic expectations is therefore causing them more emotional pain and mental turmoil than whatever problem they were originally struggling with.

*Energy*

As humans we are energetic beings. The characteristics of the energy within and around all of our bodies directly influences our ability to bring our creations to fruition.

*Our past creations are now haunting, even stalking, us!*
We need to take steps to let these go so that we have
room and permission to welcome in that which serves
us in the present moment.

*There is a need to protect and heal your creations!*
Just as our own thoughts and emotions are energies
that magnetize and attract objects of desire to us,
other people's thoughts (their goals and desires) and
emotions (their anger, concern, or jealousy) can and
most certainly do influence our ability to create. It's
important that you understand my objective in pointing this out; it's not that I want you to see yourself as
a victim, but rather I want you to see yourself as the
*master of your own universe.*

### Self-esteem
The way we perceive and feel about ourselves is a vital
ingredient (perhaps the most important ingredient)
in any alchemic recipe, yet it is consistently overlooked. In this book I will be addressing many factors
and energies that influence our capacity for self-love,
including societal ones such as capitalism, consumer-
ism, and corporate greed.

### Expansion
As our manifestation abilities increase, our creations
are growing stronger and faster; this process is creating
as much stress as it is opportunity.

### Personal vs. global

*How can we be positive about ourselves and our world when we seem to be surrounded by oceans of negativity and suffering?* Many of us feel as though we are suffering from manic-depressive disorder. One second we are feeling like masters of our own universe, meditating on the peaceful beauty of the oneness of it all. The next, we are spewing out a list as long as our grocery receipt about the unfortunate, unjust state of the world, as the pimply bagger trembles behind the five-dollar loaf of generic white bread that triggered our unseemly outburst to begin with. (Not that *I'm* ever negative, but can you believe these #*!@ prices?!)

### Note to advanced practitioners and those with short attention spans!

If any of you are thinking, *Oh, no, here we go again. If I hear, 'All you need to do is think positively and everything will be okay' one more time, I am going to puke!* you are not alone. If you have been lamenting, "I am the poster child for the law of attraction! I teach it myself! I've been saying my prayers, my affirmations, my mantras, my Hail Marys, Hail Joes, and Hail Bobs, but I still don't have the relationship I want, or the money, or that whopper of an opportunity I've been seeking, so what the hell is wrong with me?!" then you have probably experienced the law of attraction, at least in small enough doses to know there is something to it.

Otherwise, you'd be questioning the law itself. So for you, I will be brief and then get to why you may still be having problems.

### The law of attraction revisited

The main tenets of the law of attraction, found in some form in just about all the literature on the subject, are as follows:

- Your thoughts and feelings magnetize situations, objects, and people to you
- Positivity breeds positivity, negativity attracts negativity
- By raising your vibrational frequency, you attract things more quickly to yourself
- Your underlying, unconscious feelings and programming can influence your manifestations

Okay, there, I said it was going to be brief. (Those who read my first two books, including my editor, will be impressed!) Now here are some of the topics that we will expand on in subsequent chapters. I think of these as amendments, important reminders, or new takes on classic concepts. They seek to answer the questions, *Why am I having to wait so long for my wish to be granted? Why am I encountering this obstacle in my life?* and *Why doesn't the law of attraction work for me all of the time?*

- Your spirit/body connection needs to be in alignment

- You need to be anchored into your body
- Your energy as a spirit needs to be consolidated
- You need to be running your own energy in your body
- You must release your resistance to your obstacles
- You may need to forgive yourself and have more patience
- Do not rely on your creative projects to rescue you!
- Your obstacles may actually be there to propel you forward
- Your obstacles may be there to propel you in a different, better direction
- Your obstacles might be your wake-up call or even your 911 call
- Your obstacles may be forcing you to know your own strength
- Your obstacles may be giving you the experience you need to accomplish your goals
- You must rise above your own limitations by increasing your "havingness." (I will discuss havingness in more detail in chapter 10, but here's a quick definition: havingness is the extent to which a person can allow himself or herself to have abundance.)
- Different parts of yourself may be in conflict with each other, wanting different things

- Your masculine (action/logic) and feminine (intuition/receptivity) energies may be out of whack
- You may have several goals that are contradicting each other
- Your fears may be blocking you
- Your self-esteem is your greatest ally or enemy
- Your past intentions may be interfering with your present ones
- Your boredom might be creating problems in your life
- You may need to raise your energy vibration
- Your expectations may be too grounded in fantasy
- You may be too lazy! Are you seeking the easy way out or coasting through life?
- Your own time impositions may be getting in your way
- Your body or current life situation may be too out of sync with your intentions
- Your neediness may be creating an energy field you can't rise above
- Your inability to let go may be the culprit
- You may be wishing for the wrong thing—confusing the means with the end
- You may be trying to manifest something you are not yet ready for

- Your ability to manifest may be severely impacted when in relationship with others with conflicting goals (e.g., within your marriage) or within an entire society
- Someone else may be intentionally blocking you
- Someone's energy may be interfering with your own
- You may be hitting the limits of the organization you work for or belong to
- You may be stuck in a group or societal agreement that is keeping you weighed down
- You may be waiting for permission or approval from others
- You may be trying to create, as part of a couple, with someone who is not where you are at
- Your need for approval may be getting in your way

### Faith

Before I gave up my lucrative job as a federal probation officer and moved to the Philippines to study with the faith healers there, I remember wondering what the word *faith* really meant. It was a word that I found annoying, since it is used as frequently and passionately by religious fanatics as are the words *dude* and *pizza* by most teenage boys. What I came to realize is that *faith* is a word you can't really get your mind around until you've put it into practice because it's the only thing you've got left.

I was going to start this paragraph by writing, "I don't expect you to accept anything I say with faith alone," but I realized that's not true. Of course I am not asking for "blind faith." If I were, we wouldn't need to move beyond this chapter. Instead, I am asking for the kind of faith that requires you to have an inquisitive "let's try it and then wait and see" approach. If these concepts and techniques are new to you, you are going to have to have enough faith to risk taking time out of your insanely hectic schedule of working and worrying so you can practice them. What I am going to give you are the exact tools you need so that you can prove to yourself that there is in fact a genie who is standing by ready to serve you. No worries, you won't need a credit card! But she does have a few requirements if you are going to get the most out of your relationship with her. Some of these requirements include the following:

- Patience!
- The will to look honestly at yourself and those you love
- The will to allow yourself to experience and accept all of your own feelings
- The will to give up control in certain areas
- The will to take more control in other areas
- The will to let go of old thoughts and patterns

- The will to be disciplined in your thoughts and actions
- The will to put your spiritual development at the top of your to-do list
- The will to stop making excuses
- The will to stop asking others permission to be yourself
- Did I mention *patience?*

If you know you have trouble with any of the above, congratulations! You are a human being after all! The good news is that you can actually utilize the techniques in this book to increase the qualities in yourself that are currently lacking or in need of improvement. Rather than asking immediately for prosperity, you might want to focus first on manifesting courage or self-discipline or even the ability to manage your time better so that you can read and practice the exercises. For those of you who are great multitaskers, there isn't any reason why you can't work on all these things at once!

All the adversity I've had in my life, all my troubles and obstacles, have strengthened me . . . You may not realize it when it happens, but a kick in the teeth may be the best thing in the world for you.
— WALT DISNEY

# 3

# OVERCOMING RESISTANCE TO OBSTACLES

$$S = I + E + P - R$$

The strength of your manifestations, $S$, equals your clarity of intention, $I$, plus the intensity of the emotional and physical energy behind that intention, $E + P$, minus the amount of resistance, $R$.

As humans, we are massive electrical currents; and like all electrical currents, we are always seeking to complete ourselves by finding *ground* in one form or another. When we have a goal (e.g., creating a relationship), it's as if we send out a portion of ourselves that is also an electrical current that can sometimes feel as if it is stronger or even bigger than the whole of us. I believe these currents feel as if they are actually bigger than the whole of us because they are emanating from our souls. Your soul is infinitely larger and more powerful than your mind, even though most people are only or mostly aware of the mind, which is therefore the part of themselves they identify with. Alice Bailey, in A *Treatise on White Magic*, suggests that the closer we are to realizing a goal, the more intensely we desire it, and our souls have already done 90 percent of the work necessary before the desire ever enters our conscious mind. I believe she is correct.

The mind is merely the vehicle that translates the electrical current into thoughts, words, and pictures, which we then label as goals or desires. When this current moves to our heart center, emotion is added to it. This emotion is first felt as enthusiasm and excitement, which should serve as an impetus to move us forward in pursuing the goal. However, for reasons I will discuss throughout this book, we often ignore or fight against these impulses of the mind and the heart. Sometimes we do listen to them, but the enthusiasm turns to frustration or anger when the current or goal fails to reach completion. In either case, the original electrical current, now fueled or altered by negative emotion, rises up from the heart to the mind, where it is labeled as an "obstacle" or a "problem"—causing even more emotional upset. Thus a negative and unnecessary feedback loop is established until the current finds ground in the realization of the goal. I say *unnecessary* because the problem is not that the goal isn't being realized, it's that it isn't being realized fast enough as far as the mind/ego is concerned.

My goal, therefore, is to help you remain in a state of excitement over your goals by encouraging you to pursue them with absolute expectancy and patience, knowing that at the point you experience intense desire or intense pain about not having that which you desire, you are not encountering a problem, but rather a sign that the desire is close to becoming realized.

### Stop resisting!

It's often the resistance to our obstacles and our defining them as "problems" or claiming they "shouldn't be happening to us" that stops our own life force from flowing freely, which ends up causing us more distress than the problem itself. We try to ground through objects, people, and even projects to keep ourselves feeling safe. When we start even to consider letting go of these people or things, we encounter fear—even when we know this letting go is what we need to do. What or whom do *you* "ground through"?

Obstacles help propel you forward at a greater force and speed, providing you don't fall into the common trap of *resisting the resistance*, which will have the opposite effect and will slow or weigh you down even more. An obstacle is therefore not necessarily something that is in your way, but rather something that you *perceive* to be in your way. I know you already realize this, but it helps to be reminded: many obstacles, particularly the real stubborn ones, are like guardian angels. They are sent from another, wiser part of yourself to protect you or to bring you to an even better place than you could have imagined while you were in the state you were in when the obstacle popped up. On the other hand, obstacles are sometimes more a reflection of your own stubbornness or laziness than anything else.

Have you ever noticed that the more stubborn someone is, the unhappier that person tends to be, particularly when compared with someone whose mind and personality are more flexible? Most self-described stubborn people believe this trait is as unyielding as their skin color or gender. They are extremely stubborn about letting go of their stubbornness! This is unfortunate, both for them and for those in relationship with them. As much as some of you aren't going to like this, I am going to say it anyway: "stubbornness" is really a sign of egotism and immaturity. The need to be right, whether about one's life ambitions or any topic under debate, is a self-destructive psychological defense mechanism. A person who has a need to be right is likely to be a lonely person indeed.

### What does it mean to resist the resistance?
To your ego or to the analytical mind that is so desperately convinced it knows exactly what it must have and how it must have it, an obstacle is often per-

ceived as an enemy in need of immediate and absolute annihilation. Yet this perception is the true obstacle. When you are feeling frustrated, your frustration often results more from your belief that you are not getting what you want than it does from the problems arising directly from not having what you want. One part of you is feeling like it *should* be somewhere other than where it is, or it's worried that it will end up being somewhere other than where it presently is, and it is this discord that quite often creates the crisis.

### Just let go of it!

Right now I'd like you to ask yourself a question: in this very moment, how much resistance are you in? Place your hand on your heart, and ask yourself this question: how much of you and your life force are caught up in trying to fix something you perceive to be a problem, in your way, or just not right? It doesn't matter whether you are in resistance to another person or in resistance to a situation (for example, the war in Iraq, the state of your kitchen, the price of gas, your financial status, or your very own apathy, weariness, or confusion). It doesn't matter how justified you are, or feel you are, to be resisting this thing, or if you could point to millions of other people who might respond just like you. Instead, just ask yourself: how much of you is pushing or fighting against something that seems to be standing in between your peace of mind and having what you want? You might even close your eyes for a moment and visualize a gauge with an arrow. Ask the gauge to show you how much resistance you are sitting in right now, how much resistance you have to any or all of the things you would identify as obstacles.

### Ground out the resistance

A *grounding cord* is a powerful visualization tool for releasing resistance of any kind. I welcome you to imagine you are connected securely to the earth through the force of gravity. You can even visualize that, like a tree, you have a trunk running from the base of your spine deep into the planet. Imagine that any resistance you have been feeling, carrying, and sitting in is releasing down this trunk. Allow any thoughts or feelings that say, *It shouldn't be this way, There is something wrong,* or even *But you don't understand, my problems are really,* really *horrible!* to slide gently down the trunk, aided by the all-powerful force of gravity. I recommend that you perform this meditation for five minutes or longer, and then notice how you feel.

### You are fine in this moment

As you continue reading about obstacles, I encourage you to check in with yourself from time to time in this way *and* give yourself permission to release through your grounding cord, particularly when you come across a familiar scenario. I also encourage you to remind yourself, as I frequently remind myself, that right now, in this very moment, as you read this book, no matter what difficulties, dramas, or even tragedies are occurring in your life, you are just fine. You are fine even if you are reading this from the tattered seat of your dusty car, uncertain as to where you are going to sleep tonight. You are fine even if you are clinging to a bookshelf in a bookstore, where you've dragged yourself in search of the tiniest morsel of inspiration, unsure of whether you can even afford to buy this book. You are fine even if your home is going into foreclosure next week or if your spouse is going to leave you or if you are going to leave your spouse. In this very moment, as you read these words, you, *you as a spirit*, are really okay.

If you don't feel okay, then just let that feeling drop gently down your grounding cord, and breathe. Breathe it out of you and into the self-replenishing earth. Trust, even tell yourself, that by the end of this book, even by the end of this chapter, your life will undoubtedly, undeniably begin to yield unexpected and positive results through means that are taken care of for you. (For more grounding techniques and explanations, please check out my first two books!)

### Technique: Transform every worry into a happy ending

If I could give you only one simple technique, it would be this one:

As soon as you notice you are worrying, ask yourself what it is you are most worried about. What are you most fearful will happen? Once you are conscious of this fear, don't dwell on it but instead imagine the opposite outcome. For example, let's say you are worried about paying your upcoming rent. You are fearful your landlord will be angry, perhaps even evict you. Okay, stop. That's enough! Now take just a minute and visualize yourself smiling as you count out your rent in hundred-dollar bills. See yourself handing the money to your landlord and pocketing several other hundred-dollar bills as well. Imagine you are telling your friends, "Wow, that was silly for me to worry because the money flowed to me so easily, and now my landlord really loves me!" See your landlord hugging you (or buying a one-way ticket to Tahiti). Say some prayers of gratitude and conjure up feelings of relief and joy over your ability to manifest.

Doing this exercise will not only help you to create the money, but it will also provide relief from your anxiety. When you worry about lack of money, you are often suffering more from anxiety than from lack of money. Remember to utilize all your senses when using your imagination in this way: see it, think about it, feel it, and appreciate it. It doesn't matter if you can visualize in full high-definition Technicolor or if you can barely muster a cartoonish outline that fades away as soon as you create your images. Both will change your state of mind and magnetize the desired outcome to you.

The universe is full of magical things patiently waiting
for our wits to grow sharper.
—EDEN PHILLPOTTS

# 4

# WHY IS IT TAKING SO LONG?

Many of our goals take much longer than we are willing to let them take. Most of us want what we want
*now*. The idea of having to wait months if not years
for success can feel devastating. However, the more
our survival is dependent on that which we wish to
attract, the more of an urgency we will feel and the
more pressure we will put on it and ourselves. We will
be prone to slip into a fantasy world where we will
avoid making the proper wishes or taking the proper
action.

It is one thing to believe that you can manifest what you need. It's something else entirely to believe that the *one single thing* you've designated as your savior will be what actually comes to your rescue in the nick of time. This is true whether your savior is in the form of a book deal, a private investor, or Prince Charming himself. If these are what you are hoping for, what you may end up with is a couple of burly tattooed trolls with a tow truck instead, demanding that you hand over the SUV, refrigerator, or Snookums, the miniature toy poodle you bought on credit.

While I never had any possessions repossessed, I can't tell you how many times I convinced myself that I just needed to sell my screenplay or finish my book or my television pilot or start a psychic reading business right away to save me from the wrath of my landlord. My first book, *You Are Psychic*, was accepted for publication within six months after I submitted it. However, my first royalty payment didn't come for another three whole years! And that initial payment was far from the thousands I expected; rather, it was enough to fill my tank with gas. I probably wouldn't have even gotten that royalty if my own father had not preordered a few books directly from my publisher!

I am still not immune to this propensity. In order to finish this book, I needed to wipe my calendar clear of clients and students so I could really focus. I felt this would work out financially since I was told my advance would be mailed to me early in the month. However, when it did not arrive, I began to stress. I was relying on it to pay my rent for October. When weeks passed and it still wasn't here, I began sending frantic e-mails to my editor, which seemed a little strange since I am writing a book about manifesting. When I didn't hear from her (I found out she was out of town), I became even more agitated until finally I realized what I was doing and told myself, "Okay, I am going to let this go. I release my attachment to my advance and instead open the gates of possibility so that rent can pour in some other unexpected way." Not surprisingly, the day I made this decision/proclamation, money began pouring in from unexpected sources. I still had two weeks before my rent was due, but now I had everything I needed, even though the thing I was depending on originally had not arrived.

Something that helped me the most when I was down and out in Sedona (as so many other spiritual seekers are there) was meeting the legendary chanter/musician Krishna Das. While in town for the weekend, he agreed to come to my modest apartment to be interviewed for my television show, *The Psychic Explorer*. I explained to him that there were so many people in Sedona who were doing everything possible to devote themselves to their spiritual and creative work, but were having trouble surviving. I asked him if he had any advice. From the desperation he heard in my voice, I'm sure he must have known this question was more for me than anyone else. His answer was simple: "If you need money, get a job. If you're not making it with your spiritual work, do something else until you are. There is nothing spiritual about being broke."

This response from Krishna Das seemed to imprint itself deep into my brain. I've realized that it's not that we can't make a living from our spiritual or creative work—I'm finally doing just that—but that there are many factors involved, as I will discuss below. *There is no need to put pressure on the thing you love or feel compelled to do by insisting that it must be the thing that instantly supports you.* In fact, the quickest way to dry up your creative juices is to put demands on your creative projects. Yet there is also no reason why you have to wait to do the things you love until you can do them full time, or even receive any compensation for them. You can do that which you love to do and also do other kinds of work at the same time, right now!

If a full-time career zaps too much of your time and energy, you can switch to a different position or a job that requires less of an energetic commitment. Or you can find ways to incorporate your spiritual work into your mainstream job. For example, if you want to be a filmmaker, you might be able to get your employer to agree to let you make a promotional video or a documentary of a team-building retreat. If you are an energy healer, yoga teacher, or massage therapist caught in between your corporate job and your dream of owning your own business, perhaps you can begin by offering your services at the office, during lunch. If that sounds too far-fetched (it may not be for very long!), you could go get a couple of part-time jobs, which are usually less demanding. There is no reason why you have to abandon your ultimate dream. At the same time, there is no reason why your ultimate dream has to work out perfectly right now.

Many times it's not an either/or scenario. When you are ready, you can begin supplementing your work with money earned from writing, acting, boxing, healing, bungee jumping, singing, race-car driving, or anything else you love to do. As these things take off, you will naturally move toward doing them more, and pulling your energy out of work that is no longer paying off for you on a personal level.

It's quite common to experience feelings of desperation when you've left behind your old life and identity for a new one. You may be fearful that if you don't get what you want immediately, then whoever was judging you for your choices might say, "There, I told you so; you're an idiot after all." If this is the case, then just laugh at that person and your ego, and give yourself the same advice you'd give a child who is crying because he or she wants to be in second grade instead of kindergarten: be patient!

## Why we sometimes manifest goals
## that are later taken from us

You must really be capable of the opportunity you wish for!

Over a year ago I did a clairvoyant reading for a woman in her early twenties. Right away I saw a vision that told me she had outgrown her current job. I saw her visiting the offices of some executives with a portfolio under her arm, and I told her that, as unlikely as it seemed, one man looked to be offering her a management position way above the one she had now. I also saw her moving to the West Coast.

I didn't give her or the reading much more thought until she contacted me almost one year to the day later. She explained that everything I had seen had actually come to pass. However, a couple of weeks after she was offered the job (which would have paid her ninety thousand dollars per year), the company merged with another company, and someone from that other company was offered her job instead. My client was offered a position with less status and less pay that was similar to her last job, just a step above. She of course wanted to know why, at least on a spiritual level, this fantastic opportunity that she had manifested through the power of intention, good fortune, and action had been stripped away.

What I saw was that she really wasn't ready for it. She would have been in a position of supervising an entire department, and it seemed as if she hadn't quite had enough life experience that would help her be successful or cope with the pressures and responsibilities that came with this high paycheck. She admitted she had suspected the same thing, and that the woman who had been chosen from the other company had quite a bit more experience than she did. When she asked what she could do to prepare herself as quickly as possible, I got a very clear answer: "Live. Grow up." This was something she couldn't *make* happen.

I've seen many times that no matter how well versed we are in the law of attraction, we are not going to be able to manifest a particular job, an amount of money, or a joyful relationship until we have developed the skills necessary to handle it. Especially when it comes to relationships! Being a wife or even just a girlfriend is a job in itself. No matter how perfect a relationship is, there are going to be conflicts and a battle of wills—and if we don't know how to negotiate our way through these battles, the relationship is going to suffer, if not collapse. The same thing is true if you want to be in business for yourself. Until you can handle all that comes with it, you are not going to manifest a full schedule of clients. All this does not mean you shouldn't set your goals high, or give it your best effort, or avoid getting into a relationship or a new position. Go for the gold. Doing so may be the only way you can get to where you really want to be.

## Obstacles are often unconscious choices

Remember the saying "What doesn't break me makes me stronger"? Obstacles actually require us to expend extra energy. They can help us to increase our determination and the definition of what is truly important to us. For example, let's say the man you love and want to marry just got a job overseas. However, you really don't have much of an interest in leaving your own job or community. Now you seem to be caught in a terrible dilemma. What should you do? Most people would become very stressed out over this choice. However, I've discovered through my own personal experience and countless readings with people in this exact situation that most of the time, it's not about doing the "right" thing; it's about making a strong choice that will increase your commitment to a particular goal.

By choosing to give up your present life and join this man overseas, you make a strong commitment to him and your own goal of putting love and a relationship above all else. Provided that his commitment is as strong as yours is, you will most likely be successful. On the other hand, if you choose to remain where you are, perhaps to enhance your own career or because it is in the interest of your children, you are declaring to the universe, "This is what is truly important to me." This choice may very well yield greater success in your career, not just because that's where you are going to be putting your attention and time but also because there was an enormous buildup of emotional and mental energy before making the choice. This energy has now magnetized your choice, which means it will be attracting further desired experiences to you related to your choice. You are now also further along in your understanding of yourself, who you are, and what matters most. The problem occurs for people when they think that they want both things equally. However, the fact is that whatever someone ends up doing, even with a mind that complains and objects the whole way, is actually that person's true choice.

### Excuses as obstacles

I recently did a reading on a woman who very much wanted to write a book, but was convinced she didn't have time to write it, since she runs her own business and is a single mom. I asked her why she doesn't write in the evenings after her kids go to bed. She said she was too tired. I asked her why she doesn't go to sleep early and wake up early. She said she wasn't a morning person, and the kids get up early anyway. I asked her why she doesn't get up every night at midnight, write from midnight to 3:00 AM, and then go back to sleep. She then asked me why I was asking her so many stupid questions!

I suggested that perhaps she really didn't want to write a book. I told her I'd had to make those sorts of adjustments to write my first two books—and if it was possible for me, then why not for her? Was it easy? Of course not! But by making those adjustments, it eventually became possible for me to work for myself, so now I can choose to write whenever I like. So I told her that she should say, "I want to write a book, but I haven't found the discipline to do it yet" or perhaps, "Writing a book would be nice, but sleeping through the night is more important to me." These are statements no one can argue with, because they are her truth.

People who are always making excuses do so because they think their own desires and preferences are not valid enough. They use their excuses as a shield against others' disapproval or disagreement. An excuse is a type of lie. Those who utilize them are usually very transparent. They don't realize that with the excuse, they relinquish their true power. They also have to expend extra energy defending themselves from people who call their bluff.

How many people out there are using their disabilities and illnesses as excuses for letting themselves off the hook from doing jobs they hate, from giving too much of their time and energy to others, or even from having to relate to their partners on more intimate levels? I believe these excuses are why many people get sick and why they stay sick. All we have to do is look at the people with only one leg or with no legs at all who have completed marathons and triathlons to understand how nothing is impossible if we want it badly enough. The important point here is: *there is no shame in not wanting it enough.* I have far more respect for a person who says, "I don't want anything more in life than to drink beer and watch football" than I have for someone who gives me a hundred excuses for why they aren't doing more than that.

### Lack of patience is often the real obstacle!

A new client came to me recently for a psychic reading. She explained that she was having problems at work, but she did not give me any details about these problems. The first image that came to me was of her running a race. She looked quite happy until a man came up beside her, then passed her. As soon as he passed her, she halted. I addressed her in my imagination (the vehicle though which one's psychic abilities work) and asked why she was stopping, and she told me, "What's the use, he's obviously faster than me!" She then collapsed on the ground. I next asked the image to show me what would happen if she pulled herself up and continued on anyway, and I saw after a short while the other runner grew tired, slowed down, and there she was crossing the finish line.

This woman later revealed to me that she used to be on a track team but quit because she felt she wasn't the best on her team, so what was the use? She also acknowledged this was a lifelong pattern that was affecting her at work. She had been passed over for a couple of promotions and was therefore thinking perhaps she wasn't in the right place, even though she really liked it there. I felt that her answer was not to run away, or to wallow in rejection, or to get angry at her boss or the people being promoted, but to keep doing her best—and eventually she would be recognized and rewarded.

**Halfway home**
A few months ago I met with a man named Ben who seemed to be contemplating suicide. He said he was tired of trying so hard all the time to "make it" without getting anywhere. His question for me, as a psychic, was whether or not he would go to hell if he killed himself. As you can imagine, my first thought was, *Oh my God, how am I going to save him?* But as I discuss in my book *You Are Psychic*, the job of a psychic is not to judge or join the client in his or her trauma, and it's certainly not to preach one's own viewpoint (thank God the same is not true for an author!). Instead, the job of a psychic is to be as neutral as possible in order to receive the clearest, most untainted information possible. The first image I got was very clear. I saw my client hiking up an enormous mountain, looking worn out. His positioning on the mountain was what stood

out for me: he was a little more than halfway up but still had a lot farther to go.

I was reminded of times before my son was born, when I had silently implored, "Is this all there is? If so, then just let me go, God, because I think I've now experienced and learned all I possibly can." I was able to share with Ben what I have since realized: that these periods of boredom, apathy, and even depression mark the end of one phase or level of awareness followed by periods of intense change and growth, and the introduction of brand-new creative endeavors. This information seemed to give Ben encouragement, and we ended the session with his promise that he would give life another chance. Less than a month later he was unexpectedly offered a job in Hawaii, and the last I heard he was engaged to a wonderful woman he met through this new job.

## Obstacles can bump you into a brand-new direction

Several years ago during a clairvoyant reading, a client asked me to look at his business. He didn't give me any other details, and as is my usual practice, I didn't ask. Instead, I relied on my clairvoyance. The first image that came to me was of my client sitting in the driver's seat of a little toy bumper car. His car was surrounded by other bumper cars. It seemed like every time he hit another car, he was bounced backward or sideways and was facing a new direction. In this vision my client was furious, and responded by turning his car around back in the original direction, where he'd crash into yet another bumper car or into a rubbery wall off of which he'd continue to ricochet. This vision was as comical as it was perplexing.

When I asked the vision to show me what it meant, I clearly heard the word *obstacles*. The cars then turned into large hands that lifted my client up and placed him on a road that looked like a rainbow. The answer here was that if he would only choose to follow the direction he was pushed in, things would work out. If he resisted it, he would not get out of the perpetual traffic jam.

My client thought these images were funny and poignant because he had recently opened a used-car business. However, he confirmed to me that his business was not going well and that he felt that at every turn he was facing one obstacle after another—which was why he had come to me, wondering what he was doing wrong. What he was doing wrong was fighting the obstacles instead of asking himself what they were trying to tell him. Ultimately, they were telling him he was in way over his head, that he had not done the adequate planning he needed to start this business, and that it was not even one he really wanted to be in but rather what seemed like his only option after inheriting the business from his brother-in-law, who had structured it poorly himself.

**Obstacles pop up when we ignore our intuition**
How is our intuition supposed to speak to us if we refuse to listen? You might say, "God supposedly appeared to Jesus and Moses, so why doesn't God just show up in my bedroom one night and speak directly to *me?*" Well, is your mind really quiet enough to hear God's voice, or the voice of your Higher Self or soul? Are you disciplined enough to accept and respond to these voices when they may be suggesting you do exactly the opposite of what your more vociferous and obstinate ego or fears are pressing you to do? When we ignore our feminine side (intuition), it then needs to speak to us by getting our attention through our masculine (outer, physical) world.

The more we ignore the messages, the more aggressive these obstacles become. When we are completely ignoring or resisting them, their wake-up calls will turn louder and more violent, until we might actually encounter real physical harm such as accidents or illnesses. Of course illnesses can come about for any number of reasons. When they do happen, it can't hurt to ask yourself whether or not they are part of a larger message or direction that life is trying to point you in. However, the last thing you'd want to do is judge or blame yourself or anyone else for an illness.

It's unfortunate that doing so has become a prevailing attitude within many New Age communities.

## Competition with spirit

I wholeheartedly believe that we are *aspects*, *reflections*, and *co-creators* with God, whoever or whatever God is, but that many people forget the *co-* part. They want what they want when they want it, regardless of any divine plan. From my clairvoyant readings, I am beginning to believe that some people have divine plans, directives, and missions they are here to carry out, while others do not—except perhaps to live, experience life, and die. Some people convince themselves that what they are seeking is their divine plan. Sometimes it is, sometimes it's not. I believe that it's pretty obvious it's *not* their divine plan when the thing they are seeking is eluding them, if not running from them screaming (as in the case of a thwarted relationship). As adults, we are all from time to time—more often than not—a bunch of babies, screaming inwardly or outwardly because we are not getting our way fast enough.

Many people go to psychics because they say they want to know the truth. But this assertion is not true. What they want is their version of the truth confirmed. When this doesn't happen, these people blame the psychic or get very upset. Usually, the only time during a reading that people will argue with me or tell me I'm wrong is when I'm viewing their *future*—hmmm, what's that about?! The funny thing is that they usually have this reaction when I tell them I see them doing something positive and creative!

One woman told me flat-out that I was wrong when I told her I saw she would be teaching a class in her living room. She insisted she would never teach again. We laughed about this less than two months later when she began teaching a class—in her living room. Ironically, I ended up enrolling in it and she turned out to be one of the best teachers I've had. This class actually helped her pay her rent and get caught up on bills that were months behind. When she said she didn't want to teach again, what she meant was she didn't want to teach under the same circumstances as in the past. Until I offered an alternative possibility, she could not imagine anything else.

## Spirit or ego?

Quite often, the line between the yearnings of our spirit and the yearnings of our controlling ego is rather vague. I don't even know if these are two absolutely separate things, as many people propose. We tend to think they are, and judge our egos, but what is the part of ourselves doing this judging if not the ego? What is the part doing the accepting? Is the part accepting better than the part judging? If so, what part is determining that accepting is better than judging? Is that not the ego? I don't think there is anything wrong with the fact that we want what we want. But when we absolutely insist on getting it when everything in our lives is indicating it's not ours to have, or at least not yet, then *we* are the main ingredient in a recipe for disaster.

I used to work at a New Age bookstore where an older man from Australia worked as a healer. He was quite outgoing, and radiated what I would call a "guru" persona, which was partly due to a very strong love of his healing work harnessed by a hard-hitting, salesman-like approach. He guaranteed that anyone who worked with him on an ongoing basis would ascend, or at least become enlightened. (In my opinion, anyone making claims such as this should be avoided.)

He asked me if I wanted to do an exchange with him. I felt a little hesitant about this as I didn't completely trust him, but he was rather insistent and I ignored my feelings and agreed to do a reading for him. He wanted me to look at his finances and see how soon they would be improving. The images that came to me told me they were not going to improve anytime close to soon. Before telling him this, I asked the images to show me why this was. It seemed as if at one point he'd had lots of money, and it didn't look like he had been very generous with it. The message also came to me in several different ways that despite his age and self-appointed status as a spiritual leader, he was still quite a young soul, learning the meaning of humility and faith.

While I didn't dare tell him about the young soul part, I gently explained the rest. He exploded with rage! At the top of his lungs, he yelled that he had already been living in survival mode for the past three years, and he knew beyond all doubt his life was not supposed to be like this, that he had already learned all his lessons. I told him I would continue on with the reading and see if perhaps the information I was getting was wrong (thank God I knew how to ground and center myself). However, the same visions came to me again and again, confirming what I had already told him. Again he threw what looked very much like a temper tantrum. I got the strange feeling that he wasn't arguing with me at all, but rather with himself and with his God. I don't know exactly what his definition of being enlightened was, but if this was a display of it, I don't think I'd want to go there!

**Stubborn people manifest stubborn obstacles!**
The more stubborn you are, the more you will get stuck. When you get stuck, you will really be stuck. People with strong personalities are often strong alchemists who really have to look out for and listen to their own feelings, because their feelings will start manifesting for them in very extreme and powerful ways. I had a student like this. Whenever I did readings on her, I was

awestruck by the amount of energy her body generated. She had been overweight her entire life, and I really think that was partially the reason for all this energy. Her body was a mega-energy machine. She had some pretty strong ideas about what she wanted for herself and a lot of fear about what might happen if she didn't get what she wanted. The problem was this: as soon as she felt unhappy about a situation, her being said, "I want out of here!" even though her brain was saying, "You have to stay here in this miserable, abusive situation." She would therefore begin to manifest situations (i.e., drama) that forced her out, such as accidents that left her disabled and unable to do her work, or people who would become angry at her and end up firing her.

Whenever I did a reading for her, I would see that these situations were projections from herself trying to push her in a direction that would make her happier. Had she just been able to allow herself to be in the flow of wisdom and grace, she wouldn't have had to go through such trauma and drama before getting to where she truly needed to be. Once she could own her constant problems as her own manifestations, she was able to feel less of a victim, although it took her about a decade to really get this.

In light of knowledge attained, the happy achievement seems almost a matter of course, and any intelligent student can grasp it without too much trouble. But the years of anxious searching in the dark, with their intense longing, their alterations of confidence and exhaustion, and the final emergence into the light—only those who have experienced it can understand that.
— ALBERT EINSTEIN

# 5

# WHAT DO YOU REALLY WANT?

**Don't confuse the means with the ends!**
One of the criticisms of the recent law-of-attraction mania is that there is too much focus on money and prosperity. While I think that some of this judgment, if not most of it, is coming from people who themselves are not financially well off or are suffering from being trapped beneath a ceiling of their own limitations, it is important to understand that money is just one of the many things that we can attract into our lives, and that money is never the be-all and end-all.

When we have a need or desire for more money, it is very important that we be clear about what we hope to achieve by accumulating this additional money. Many people want to be rich, because they think wealth will free them from a boring job, free up their time, make it possible for them to travel, or allow them to be more creative or drive a nice car. Money may help with these things, or it may not. Many people say they want to travel and actually do possess the money to do so, but they either don't make the time or they can't figure out where to go or whom to go with. If you want more than anything to travel and you really are able and willing to allow yourself to have this goal, you will have an easier time manifesting a trip even if at this moment you don't have a dollar, as opposed to someone who has millions but is struggling with something inside themselves that won't allow them this time off.

Many people want to have plenty of money so they can feel secure and ward off feelings of fear. While money can make it easier to do these things, it may not be the answer. A fearful, anxious person is not going to become happier through having money any more than a person who feels undeserving and bad about themselves is. Fearful people may in fact accumulate money because they are more likely to do everything possible to have a stable income; however, such people will sacrifice their own happiness by putting up with things not in their best interest. The person who feels undeserving may be able to manifest money but won't be able to hold on to it for very long.

One of the most important things you can do for yourself when seeking more money, or seeking to manifest a certain goal, is to ask yourself what steps you can begin to take *today* regardless of your situation. Many of us use lack of money as an excuse for not taking care of ourselves. It's a very convenient excuse, but as long as you hold it, you are not going to have money or the things you really crave.

### EXERCISE
## Understanding your true goals

Separate a piece of paper into seven rows. In the first row, write your most pressing goal or wish. Then ask yourself, what end will this goal achieve or why do you desire this? Write the answer in the second row. In the third row, rewrite the goal to include the reason you want to achieve what you just wrote in row 2. Then look at your answer and redetermine what it is you really need or want. You can record this response in the fourth row and label it your final goal. In the fifth row, you can include specific details about the reworked goal; and in the sixth row, restate your wish as an intention. In the seventh row, state how this will make you feel and make a declaration that you have already manifested your goal. You can include emotions along with your intentions, too. Here's an example:

| 1. Goal/wish | Money |
|---|---|
| 2. What will this achieve? Why do I desire this? | Money will make it possible for me to buy a new car. |
| 3. Reason I want to achieve what I just wrote in row 2 | I want a new car so I will have a reliable, comfortable, fun way to get around. |
| 4. Rewrite goal as the final goal | What I really want is a car. |
| 5. Specific details of this goal | The car will be safe, run perfectly, have air conditioning, and be in a color that makes me happy. |
| 6. Restate your wish as an intention | I intend to manifest a great car with all the features I would love. |
| 7. State both the emotion you feel and the certainty you have already manifested your goal | I feel so very joyful, excited, relaxed, and at ease knowing this car has already manifested for me, so now I am just waiting for it to arrive. |

From this exercise, you will be able to reword and formulate your goals so that they best suit what you are really seeking. There is nothing wrong with desiring money for the sake of having money. However, if the thing you really need right then, which most of your life force is going to, is something other than money, you may be limiting the way it comes to you by focusing on money or obtaining credit rather than the thing itself, which in this case is a dependable, affordable, and attractive car. A car can be given to you, it can be loaned to you, or you can come across an amazing bargain (as I just did with my Mercedes-Benz). All these things can happen for reasons you never imagined, while you were trying to figure out how on earth you were going to manifest it.

By focusing on the end result as opposed to the way in which it comes to you, you open up many more creative possibilities for yourself and bypass the limits your logical mind normally encounters.

### Relationships
Let's look at another common goal: relationships.

| 1. Goal/wish | To have Brad Pitt as my boyfriend |
|---|---|
| 2. What will this achieve? Why do I desire this? | If I have Brad Pitt, I'll have a really cute, sexy guy to have fun with, who will take me to exotic, exciting places. |
| 3. Reason I want to achieve what I just wrote in row 2 | I don't want to be lonely anymore. I want excitement, fun, and romance, but also a guy who is there for me every night and every day, whom I can trust and depend on. |

| 4. Rewrite goal as the final goal | I want a man described as above so I will get to experience what a committed, loving relationship is about while also being more happy in my life. |
|---|---|
| 5. Specific details of this goal | He will be sexy, fun-loving, caring, handsome, and exciting, and also stable and committed. He will love me with all his heart and be completely available. |
| 6. Restate your wish as an intention | I intend to manifest a great relationship with a man I love and who loves me, who is completely available in every sense of the word. |
| 7. State both the emotion you feel and the certainty you have already manifested your goal | I feel so very joyful, excited, relaxed, and at ease knowing this relationship has already manifested for me—and now I am just waiting for it to arrive. |

From the example above, you can see that who you are wishing for is not necessarily Brad Pitt, as you may have initially listed in the first row, but instead a relationship with a person who will bring the qualities to your life that you believe Brad Pitt embodies. The fact is, the actor Brad Pitt is committed to another woman. He is therefore not available right now in the way you need him to be. If you are seeking a man who will be there when you come home, then Brad isn't who you want.

Not to say Brad Pitt wouldn't be interested in you; maybe he would. I dreamed about a date with him recently (please don't tell my boyfriend!). He was actually very polite, and he even bought me champagne when all I could ask for was a beer; however, the idea of him comparing me to Angelina kind of put a damper on things, even though she wasn't around. I also dated Tom Cruise in a dream last week. He was nice, but I hurt his feelings when I left without saying goodbye, which I did because I didn't realize he'd care. Hmmm, do you think I need to work on my self-esteem, too?

The example above actually includes two wishes, which is fine but does complicate things. The fact is you might be wishing for a relationship *and* more fun and excitement. Or, what you might really be seeking is fun and excitement, but you erroneously believe that the only way you can have these experiences is with a relationship. In this case you might break these goals into two, so you can show yourself that the two don't have to be paired together. That way, if it takes longer to manifest the relationship, you won't have to put off having the fun and excitement you seek or vice versa.

I've seen in my work with so many clients that the reason they weren't manifesting any relationship was because they wanted to hold out for "the one." These people were getting discouraged because of large gaps in between significant relationships, and they wondered what was wrong with them. What usually came up was that they had made a strong agreement with themselves that they would not accept anything less than "the one," and so these people experienced a longer gap in between significant relationships compared to others who felt a need to fill that space with any relationship. It helps to understand that most of the time we are getting exactly what the strongest part of ourselves most desires.

### When your soul mate dumps you

Far too many people, particularly women, refuse to exchange their fairy-tale fantasies for a realistic picture of a situation. They are so focused on the feelings a person elicits within them, or so stuck on the idea that this person is the only one who can save them from the rest of their miserable lives, that they refuse to accept the facts of the present moment, which are quite often that the object of their desire is not available or not interested in them or both. Many women have relationships with their fantasy of a man rather than the man who actually exists. They will give every ounce of their energy to this man, when he may have never given them anything more than a smile, a compliment, or a healing session.

The New Age concept of the soul mate has exacerbated this problem. In the past, to give up Prince

Charming meant to risk being lonely or broke. Today the stakes are higher: to give up the one you or the psychic on the boardwalk has identified as your "soul mate" or "twin flame" suggests you might very well be damned for the rest of this life, if not for all of eternity! Never mind if the guy won't return your calls, refuses to ask you on a date, or is married with six kids and hasn't given any indication he's ever going to leave his wife.

I am not downplaying the possibility that we have attachments to people based on past-life agreements. I am saying that you can create the relationship you think you want, but you can't have every person you think you want, even when your feelings for them are intense or you had a close connection to them in the past. Most people's problems in relationships stem from the discrepancy between what is and how they hoped or expected things to be. By reorienting yourself to what is and what it is you really want, it becomes easier to let go of the person you never even had.

### Security

Let's look at one more common goal and dilemma for many people:

"I want security, but the only way to have security is to have a nine-to-five job with a good pension plan for the next twenty years. However, I'm tired, I hate my job, and I want to be free."

| 1. Goal/wish | Financial security |
|---|---|
| 2. What will this achieve? Why do I desire this? | It will ensure I have money for the rest of my life so I can live well. It will ensure I don't have to feel stressed out about money or ever be without it. |
| 3. Reason I want to achieve what I just wrote in row 2 | I don't want to ever be without money because that state is too stressful and scary. The thought of not being able to pay my rent or becoming homeless is just too awful. But so is the idea that I may have to work jobs I hate for the next twenty years. |
| 4. Rewrite goal as the final goal | I always want to have a great place to live, to not feel stressed but instead confident I am always okay, and I want to do the things I love and feel excited about. |
| 5. Specific details of this goal | I will always be able to live in a fantastic home, and I will live a joyful life. |
| 6. Restate your wish as an intention | I intend to manifest multiple ways to always be able to live in a place that feels safe, peaceful, and happy to me, and at the same time I will be happy on a daily, even minute-to-minute basis, always doing what I love. |
| 7. State both the emotion you feel and the certainty you have already manifested it | I feel very joyful, excited, relaxed, and at ease knowing that I will always be able to live in a fantastic place, and I will always do what I love to do the most on a minute-to-minute basis. |

You will notice in this example that I left things very wide open. I didn't say, "I always want to find a way to pay my rent," because the fact is that maybe someday I will own a house or maybe someone will give me a house to live in rent-free. I didn't say, "I will have a great job," because maybe someday very soon I won't have a job but will instead work for myself, or perhaps I won't have to work at all. In fact, the word *work* can have so many negative connotations that I might choose to leave it out of my goals entirely and instead replace it with the word *create*.

I wrote, "I will always do what I love." This opens up a myriad of possibilities. Perhaps what you will eventually discover is that you'd love to sail around the world, or adopt a child, or work in an orphanage in Bangladesh, or become a psychic or an architect or the vice president of the United States! We want to leave a lot of possibilities open for ourselves, but at the same time get very specific about the qualities, emotions, and end result of whatever experiences come our way.

**Body, weight loss, and exercise:
You must be willing to do whatever it takes**
When I use the phrase *absolutely everything*, I'm including both physical action and the inner work of the spirit/mind.

If you have not yet achieved your picture of success, ask yourself the following questions:

- Am I doing absolutely everything in my power to develop my talents?
- Am I doing absolutely everything in my power to meet the right people?
- Am I doing absolutely everything I can do to make this goal happen?
- Am I willing to do all the steps to get to my ultimate goal?
- Are there conditions attached to what I am willing to do for this?
- How can I volunteer my time or make contributions in this area, so that I can meet people, learn, and help others?
- Am I in the best shape physically to achieve this goal?
- Am I living in the best place to achieve my goal?
- Have I let go or detached enough energetically, psychologically, and physically from all those people who might want to stop me from achieving my goal?

If you can't answer yes to all of these questions, then there is a part of you that doesn't want this thing as much as you think you do. Instead, the desire to sleep more, have an easier time, to have others take care of you, and to be comfortable is stronger than this goal is for you. Once you have this awareness, you are no longer powerless, because now you know you are really getting what you want. This then makes it easier to make a new choice when you are motivated to do so.

For a long time I thought I wanted to lose weight and eat healthier. But what I really wanted more was to eat junk food, steak and potatoes, and chocolate. I wanted to eat out at restaurants and sit down to meals with my family where we all ate the same delicious food. I discovered these were the things I wanted more than losing weight because these were the things I was *choosing* to do. At the same time, another part of me felt powerless and not in control of my own body, and that didn't feel good.

Eventually I decided I wanted to get in shape and lose weight more than I wanted free grazing time in the kitchen. As I will discuss in chapter 17, this decision corresponded with the arrival of the perfect opportunity to help me achieve this goal. What helped me the most was to shout out a proclamation every time I was offered or came across something not on my diet. What I yell out is, "I am stronger than this french fry!" This provides endless amusement for my son, who just can't wait to see whether or not his mom is actually stronger than a french fry or a hamburger or a Snickers bar. Most of the time I am, but sometimes, well, come on, it's just one tiny little bite!

The other thing I do when I come across something that violates my diet is to take a few seconds to make a conscious choice. I will remind myself that I can eat this now, or I can fit into whatever I choose to wear in four months. I can drink this now, or I can prepare myself for the television pilot that I am sure will manifest by the time I'm at my goal weight. Which would I prefer? If I forget to do this evaluation and start chomping away, I will actually spit out the food and then do the evaluation. Taking a few extra seconds to make these choices is really working in conjunction with the diet and exercise program I am following. And it only took about a month and eight pounds to slip away before I got a call for a TV pilot!

This practice can be done in many areas in which you may be facing two courses of action that seem to contradict each other.

To see a world in a grain of sand and a heaven in a wild flower,
Hold infinity in the palm of your hand
And eternity in an hour.
—WILLIAM BLAKE

# 6

# CREATIVE ENERGY AND THE CLAIRVOYANT TECHNIQUE

The powers of creation and destruction exist within every human. It's my personal belief that it is our own spirit-souls that manifest themselves through the creation of the physical body. In other words, you are the creator of your body and much of the world you live in. Before birth, throughout your life, and after death, you have the ability to mold your body and your immediate surroundings into just about any form that you can first imagine.

In an instant, at every instant, we have the power to reshape, even destroy, our sculpted artistic creations, which include our own body, mind, and personality, or any material object on this planet. In this analogy, we are constantly mixing our own little lumps of clay with those of everyone around us. Sometimes in this process, our portions become indefinable, even lost; sometimes they grow larger and more stunning than we ever expected. Perhaps ultimately, we join back up with that original massive lump of clay in the sky we call God or heaven.

### Acknowledging our small creations first

At every waking or sleeping moment we cannot help but create or manifest something. This something starts with a thought, a wish, or a desire that may be conscious or unconscious. A conscious desire would be: *I am thirsty, I want something to drink.* We then pull our little buns out of bed, stumble to the refrigerator, and within a minute or two are guzzling down a refreshing glass of chocolate milk (soy or rice milk for you vegans out there).

"So what? I got myself a glass of milk!" you might say. "I did not produce the carton of chocolate milk, I did not milk the cow—heck, my wife did the shopping, so I didn't even buy it." But the fact remains: one moment it wasn't in your life or your tummy, and through the simple process of wishing, thinking, and

taking a series of simple actions to fulfill that desire—
you suddenly have this something that wasn't yours
before: a glass of chocolate milk.

Take a good look around you. What do you see?
A TV set, a window, the view behind the window,
your cell phone on the end table, your cat, your husband, and your husband who is now drinking your
glass of milk and switching the channel on your TV
since you took your attention off of it for half a second. These are all your beautiful, wondrous creations
that would not be in your life had you not invited
them in through your expectations, your choices, your
thoughts, and your actions. Did others have a hand in
forming or bringing these creations to you? Of course
they did! But that doesn't negate the fact that every
single thing you can sense—from the nail polish on
your toes to the birds chirping outside your window—
is part of your experience because of your wishes and
choices.

The point here is that you have already exercised
your creative power a million times over. Therefore,
manifesting anything consciously, no matter how
large you deem it to be, is not that far-fetched. Every
time we contemplate and appreciate our past successes
with manifesting, it becomes easier to utilize the law
of attraction.

**The classic clairvoyant manifestation technique**

The following exercises involve the use of visualization, clairvoyance, and healing for the purpose of manifesting. They address the fact that everything we manifest on the physical plane begins as energy, which is then directed by thought and emotion, and channeled into a picture that reproduces itself on the physical plane. Sometimes this energy is contaminated or too weak, and therefore it either cannot manifest into the physical or it manifests as an inferior and ultimately less desirable form. When this happens, most people try to make changes on the physical plane rather than starting with, or going back to, the original blueprint.

Most people aren't aware of energy dynamics. They aren't aware of the original energy blueprint or that they were the original architects of the blueprint. They therefore don't realize that they are always free to destroy it and start over, or make adjustments to it that will then be reflected within their creations that show up in their lives. An example of this would be someone who has been thinking about how much he or she needs a car. When the car shows up, it has some major flaws. In this example, the person who is not aware of energy will just put up with the car until the car falls apart, or will spend time and money to fix up the car or to go search for the right car.

What such people don't realize is that instead of taking physical action, they may be better served by turning inward to their personal drawing or drafting boards and modifying or completely revamping their blueprint, which could potentially deliver a better car to their doorstep within minutes.

The following techniques utilize visualization, clairvoyance, and healing. Visualization is using the power of intention to conjure up images and colors in your imagination. This is where you give your mind the command to imagine something. Clairvoyance is a psychic ability that allows you to receive information in the form of images and colors. It is passive or receptive so that you command your mind to wait and see what shows up, and quite often what shows up is not what you expected. Healing is manipulating the images you've created through visualization, or received through your clairvoyance, in order to achieve a state of health or a desired outcome. When these three modalities are used together, just about anything can be achieved.

These techniques are similar to those that have been utilized by thousands of psychics and alchemists for decades. Because they work so well, these techniques are currently taught in numerous clairvoyance training schools throughout North America.

EXERCISE

## Creating and clearing an energetic blueprint

1. See a clear, transparent rose out in front of you. Let this rose represent yourself. Make a wish and put it into this rose by visualizing a symbol for your wish (e.g., a diamond, a man, a check for $100,000) and dropping this symbol in the rose. Notice if the rose turns any colors or changes in any way once you put the symbol inside the rose. If you don't spontaneously see a color, then assign it one that makes you feel happy.

2. Next, inside the rose, visualize a little scene with you receiving the symbol and feeling overjoyed that you have received it. See yourself taking some celebratory actions as a result of having received it. See yourself benefiting from this thing you have now allowed yourself to receive.

3. Next, let the stem of the rose form a grounding cord that plants the rose firmly into the earth. Ask for a color to appear that represents any resistance to you having this goal, whether coming from yourself or from someone else. This color may emerge within the color you saw or chose in step 1. Let the force of gravity suck out any of the colors that appeared when you invited the resistance to show itself. Once you feel that the rose contains only your own

energy, see this color of your own energy growing brighter and stronger until it's sparkling brilliantly from the rose in all directions. Cut the stem and let the rose either rise up into the hands of God or out into the universe to begin manifesting for you.

### Birthing your desired symbol

Hold your hands over your womb. Visualize a crystal flower in your womb, or where your womb would be if you were a woman and had a womb. Within the crystal flower, place a symbol for the thing you desire to birth. Once you have that image, conjure up some emotions with the help of thoughts of appreciation and future memories of what a terrific time you are having. Then invite the creative energy within your womb to begin circulating through the flower with its symbols, energizing it. See a color for that energy beaming out from the flower inside your womb, which will further activate that part of your body. Once you feel as if you've accomplished this, than let the flower come out of your womb and imagine you are now holding it in your hands. Imagine it is sprouting wings and flying away to begin to manifest for you.

### Healing your creative energy

Within your body exists a wellspring of creative energy. This energy seems to coalesce within the area of the reproductive organs. When people are attracted to each other, it's often this part of the body that becomes activated. This is also where people tend to cord energetically into each other. For example, if a man becomes sexually aroused by thinking about a particular woman, some of his sexual energy will travel over to the woman, who will receive it within her reproductive centers. The man's sexual energy may then actually stimulate her own, even if the man and woman are standing in different rooms.

The same process occurs with emotions. If someone is angry or sad and thinking about another person, then those thoughts become conductors through which the emotion can flow right to that other person. When that other person receives the emotions, he or she will not usually understand where it came from. Unfortunately, since most people don't understand how this process works, they believe any emotion they are feeling must come from their own self.

Ironically, most people seek to heal their own emotions (or sexual arousal) by searching for an outside source that will seemingly give them justification for experiencing whatever they are feeling, so they will then blame whoever is in their immediate environment. For example, let's say my sister is having a really bad day and she starts thinking that maybe she should talk to me to feel better, but for whatever reason doesn't even get around to calling me. I might suddenly start feeling anxious and cranky. Then, if I don't know or even suspect that I've begun channeling her emotions, I might start asking myself whether I have a chemical imbalance. Or my son might walk into the room and throw his towel on the floor, and I will decide that his behavior must be the source of my crankiness. I will therefore reprimand him more harshly than I usually would. In this way, we pass on our emotions to others like viruses, both through energy exchanges and through direct action. Those who are closest to us, those whom we love the most, are the ones who frequently suffer the most. This is particularly true when an energetic connection has previously been established, through sexual activity or through the birth process.

### Types of energy problems

Many of the problems people have with manifesting their wishes and goals have to do with the level and quality of creative energy that is stored within their own body. If you think of this energy as a fuel source for your body, as gasoline is for a car, it's easier to understand how things can sometimes go wrong. With a car:

- There may not be enough fuel
- The car may be leaking fuel

- You may have put in too much fuel
- You may not be using the best fuel for the car—it could be too strong or too weak
- You may be driving the car in a way that is not maximizing the fuel in the car
- Someone else might be driving your car
- You might be trying to run the fuel through the wrong parts of the car

The good news is that, unlike the fuel in your car, your creative fuel won't cost you a penny once you allow yourself to have it! Most importantly, it's never too late to get it back.

### Do you have leakage?

Many people leak out their creative/sexual energy all over the place. Where does it go when it leaks? Most often it goes directly to someone whom the person desires or who desires the person. People with this type of leakage problem often struggle with boundary issues. They may also struggle with promiscuity, infidelity, or commitment. This problem is often related to the following:

### Trying to run the fuel through the wrong parts

Much of the way we run or fail to run our creative energy is patterned after the way our parents ran their energy or put a clamp on our own. Many young people never have the slightest idea that they have a creative bone in their body, because such creativity was something their own parents either stifled or ignored in themselves. Teenagers often believe that a sexual or romantic object is the only interesting place into which to channel their creative energy. This is a setup for disaster, because the blossoming adults confuse the power of their creative energy with the power of the object of their desire, and more and more energy goes into pursuing this object. This can set young adults up for a lifetime of unfulfilling relationships, as they desperately search to find the creative energy they have transferred from themselves to their fantasy of the other person—which is also one reason a person can become really obsessed with another. What such people don't realize is that the excitement, passion, exhilaration, health, joy, and peace that they are seeking is available to them not through another person, but from fully embracing their own creative life force.

If this possibly describes or resonates with you to any extent, I highly recommend doing the following exercise. You can do this exercise either by sitting with your eyes closed, or by sitting or standing in front of a mirror, wearing comfortable clothes that make you happy.

- Put your hands over your womb. If you are a man, you can imagine you have a womb. (Don't worry, this will be our little secret!)

- Declare that you are now calling all your creative life-force energy back to you.
- Visualize your womb filling up and getting bigger and bigger as you bring the energy back, so that you resemble a pregnant person.
- Ask your womb to show you the color of your creative life-force energy.
- Let this energy redistribute itself wherever it would like to flow throughout your body.

### If you lack creative energy

- Do the exercise above, and then add the following steps:
- See a gauge with an arrow that can move from 1 to 100, and imagine that the number at which it is set represents how much permission you have to run your own creative life-force energy.
- If the gauge is at any less than 90, imagine you are lifting the arrow until it gets to the number you'd like.
- Imagine you are placing this gauge in your womb. Now invite the creative energy to begin brewing, as if the few cells that contain it are now being activated and tons of this energy are exploding from the cells, filling up this entire part of your body and then expanding to every other cell in your body. Let this energy expand

from the cells throughout every system in your body, from the circulatory system to the sympathetic and parasympathetic nervous systems. Let it wash through your bones and muscles and face and hands and legs and out the top of your head, forming a beautiful fountain that then washes through your aura, the energy field surrounding your body.

- Make sure you let this creative energy wash through your heart and down your shoulders, down through your underarms, through your forearms and wrists, bubbling out your hands like fountains. In your imagination, flush your entire lymphatic system with this cleansing energy color.

### If you have too much creative energy

Sometimes you can have so much creative energy running through your body that it becomes almost too much to bear. In such a case, you will either get sidetracked from whatever you're trying to achieve or you'll begin to create more than you can handle at one time. For example, you may begin to take on far too many projects or overcommit yourself to too many people. Moreover, too much creative energy running through your body will tend to push your spirit out. When you are too far out of your body, you may begin to experience symptoms such as restlessness, nervousness, feeling overwhelmed, spaciness, and having trouble sleeping or focusing on any one thing for very long. In the next chapter I will discuss this issue in more detail.

### If you have too much sexual energy

When creative energy is channeled primarily through the sexual organs and/or objects of sexual attraction, it can be extremely distracting and uncomfortable—and cause people to make choices that are not in the best interest of themselves or others. Sometimes it makes them act out sexually in inappropriate ways. People who run too much sexual energy for too long might end up with health problems in this area, in the way that a device running on a battery that's too charged or too strong might burn out some of the other electrical components. I believe that our creative energy is made of the same stuff as our sexual energy; it's just that our sexual energy runs primarily through the sexual organs.

Sometimes when we are feeling completely out of control about a particular person or relationship, it is because this person is energetically corded into our sexual organs. We feel out of control because this person's energy doesn't belong to us, but we don't know that, so we are perplexed about why we can't stop it. (The same can be said about another person's emotions, such as anger or grief.) When this happens, we experience the other person's vibrational frequency as our own, so that in the case of sexual energy it may actually feel as intense as if we were having physical contact. This energy exchange can happen with those we desire, and even those we'd prefer to avoid! Tantra practitioners utilize this exchange consciously to enhance their sexual experiences, whereas the rest of the population benefits and suffers without much awareness.

This exchange is often also accompanied by thoughts that have been sent by the other person, usually unconsciously but sometimes on purpose. The problem here is many people will then follow the will of the one sending the energy, which can get in the way of their own good judgment. Once this energy connection is broken, interest in the other person or willingness to be with that person often disappears and is replaced by feelings of self-condemnation and thoughts that go something like, *Oh my God, how could I have ever considered sleeping with that jerk for even a second?* Many people then blame this "error in judgment" on alcohol.

EXERCISE

## Grounding your reproductive organs

The solution to running too much energy or someone else's energy through your own body? Ground your ovaries or testicles! This might sound funny, but it really works!

Sit down in a chair with your feet touching the ground. Put your hands over your ovaries if you are a woman. If you are a man, place your hands over your testicles. In your imagination, see a very strong column of energy running from your ovaries or testicles straight down, deep into the earth. Invite the force of gravity to extract any excess or foreign energy your body can't handle. You can really do this anytime during the day, not just when you are sitting alone; you can even do it while you are conversing with someone else!

Enlighten the people generally, and tyranny and oppression of body
and mind will vanish like evil spirits at the dawn of day.
— THOMAS JEFFERSON

# 7

# HEALING THE BODY/SPIRIT CONNECTION

From the thousands of readings I've done, I've observed
that people who tend to be more prosperous than the
rest of us have three things going for them:

1. They are fully integrated/connected/anchored
   into their body.

2. The life-force energy that runs through their
   body is vibrant and compact.

3. Their auras appear larger than the auras of less
   prosperous people.

The good news is there are simple exercises you can do to obtain these qualities, which you will find at the end of this chapter.

Fortunately, all of these qualities can be enhanced through intention and visualization.

### Integration of body and spirit

I went for a while being broke after my son was born. During this particularly bumpy time, I sought out readings from several clairvoyant friends. I always asked the psychic/clairvoyant/channeler of the week to "look" and see when my millions would be coming in; no fewer than three of these people, all of whom resided in different states and did not know each other, told me the problem was that there was more of me outside of my body than in it. They each saw a similar vision of me floating out among the clouds, in a dreamy state. They could see I was diligently sending out intentions through visualizations and affirmations, yet somehow I wasn't materializing what I wanted because not enough of me was on the material plane and because I was too spread out all over the place.

Since that time I've done readings for quite a few clients who also struggle with being "spread too thin" or disconnected from their body. It's not just that they are doing too many things at once, or that their attention is shifting from one thing to the next without clear focus. It's as if a part of them, their spirit, is either too diffused, or too far away from the body. The opposite of this would be those who appear as consolidated beams of light.

*Symptoms:* Are you having trouble meeting your own basic survival needs? If so, do you find yourself feeling confused, exhausted, and unable to focus on any one thing? Do you feel detached, with an unreal or dreamy feeling? Do you find you are always thinking about the past or planning/trying to figure out the future? Does a part of you long to be free from the trials and tribulations of the physical body? Do you feel as though it's not fair that your own survival needs even have to be an issue? Have you experienced illness, or have you been in pain or undergone a shocking or traumatic experience lately that has impacted you? Do you feel that you know what you don't want but not what you *do* want, aside from some nebulous idea of wealth so you never have to think about money again?

**To be in or out of the body; that is the question**
If you've been spending more time out of your body than in it, or if you are depleted or too dispersed all over the place, you may need to make adjustments to get yourself back into balance. This doesn't have to be a long, arduous task. Sometimes the answer is just to get more sleep and give your body more of what it wants, such as exercise and healthy, nutritious food.

Clearing out your house of everything that is no longer making you happy can also help your body/spirit connection. People tend to leave or stay away from their body when there is too much pain within it, or their physical circumstances are unpleasant. So, alleviating these issues can help draw you back in.

It is important to understand that there are valid reasons for leaving your body. We do it every night when we're sleeping. We obviously need sleep, quite often more than we get. In fact, researchers who attempt to go without sleep for even a few days begin showing signs of psychosis. When you sleep, your spirit is often very busy working out problems, healing the body, and downloading information. The same is true when you leave your body during waking states. Highly artistic people usually spend a lot of time out of the body. However, the artists who make money from their art are those who can come back in and connect deeply with the body when doing so is called for.

### EXERCISE
### Discover where you are in relation to your body

Collect yourself up into your solar plexus. See yourself as a ball of energy. Notice or choose a color that represents you as spirit. Imagine you are rising up to your heart, then throat, then head, then above your head. Go up to the ceiling and land on a light fixture there.

If there is none, imagine you are hanging out in the corner of the room. From this position, imagine you are looking back at your body, but don't return to it yet. Instead, visualize a tape measure and imagine you are measuring the distance between where you are on the ceiling and where your body is.

Next, imagine you are moving up above the ceiling onto the roof. Once again, get out your trusty little tape measure and measure the distance from the roof to your body. Now go up to the nearest cloud and take a measurement, then continue on to the farthest cloud, then to the edge of the atmosphere, then to a distant planet of your choice. Once on that planet, measure the distance from there to your body.

Next, create a gift for your body such as a bouquet of flowers or a sparkling jewel, and send it back down to your body so that this mental gift will land right inside the top of your head and down to your heart. See if you can actually keep your focus from the farthest-away point as you acknowledge your body down below. Now follow this gift all the way back down, passing or resting at the places you stopped at on your way up and out. When you get back to your body, enter it through your crown and move to your heart. Notice how it feels in there.

Place your hand on your heart to make sure you are really there—behind your hand, inside your body. Now, move back up to your sixth chakra, behind your third eye. Imagine you can open that eye and look out. Next, form a connection with a very heavy cord between the base of your spine and the earth. Open your eyes and look around. Things might look a little different now. Observe the objects in the room as though it's the first time you've really looked at them. Remind yourself you are now going to be completely, 100 percent present with yourself.

**The strength and size of your energy field**
Some people seem to have very strong, hearty spirits. Clairvoyantly, their spirits look larger than others. These people seem to be able to manifest money more easily than those whose spirits appear smaller, or whose life force, which I see as light, is dimmer. These latter folks appear small or dim, and they tend to suffer from exhaustion, depression, and a variety of illnesses.

Other people actually seem to have an overabundance of life-force energy. These folks usually can't sit still for very long and are likely to be diagnosed with "attention deficit disorder" early on in life. Depending on their level of physical activity, they will often struggle with weight problems. If you think about the most hyper child you've seen, quite often that child has three problems on an energy level. First, their spirit is often too big for their little body to handle. Second, they are often running too much of someone else's energy through their body (e.g., their parents' emotions), which makes them act like mini-versions of the Incredible Hulk. The third problem is that these kids are often completely ungrounded, having one foot, so to speak, in the body, and the other zooming out all over creation. Stick that kid in a classroom or his bedroom and leave him to his own devices, and the room will soon look like a bomb shelter attacked from the inside, with the adult no longer in charge looking like a survivor of a nuclear attack.

Many of these children/spirits eventually grow into their body or learn to cope with it. They learn to ground, focus, and channel their excess energy into productive means. Others end up using drugs, prescription or illicit, in order to deal with the discrepancy of having too much or not enough of their own energy in their body. If you look at people like Oprah Winfrey, Tom Cruise, Elton John, Hillary Clinton, or Barack Obama, you will see people who have managed to harness their own power and achieve what others would never even dare for themselves. If adults are not able to find firm grounding or focus, their excess energy/power may over-energize their emotional body, which will propel them from one personal crisis to another, like an out-of-control steam engine barreling down diverging tracks.

## Stress relief 101—consolidating all the *yous*

This is a terrific meditation when you are feeling over-whelmed! I developed it when I thought I was about to have a nervous breakdown, when I saw hundreds of "me"s all over the place, attached to one body that had no idea which direction to go in first.

Get out some paper and take no more than a few minutes to write down your to-do list for the next six months. This list should include everything you are responsible for on a daily basis as well as special projects. If there's too much, you can write down categories instead, such as "Respond to e-mails," "Call everyone back," "Clean the house," and so on, mixed in with some individual tasks.

Next, put this list aside and go into a meditative space. Close your eyes. Ask yourself, "If my anxiety were located at a certain point in my body, where would that be?" Then postulate that point is where you are going to center yourself for the rest of the exercise. Next, imagine that you are looking at a screen out in front of you, spanning 360 degrees around your head. Allow yourself to see a version of yourself engaging in each one of these tasks. You will most likely see several copies of yourself, all doing things. Make a mental note of where they are on your screen—e.g., you taking out the trash might be to the left, you giving a presentation might be to the right; then, if you have three kids, there might be three of you driving the kids to soccer practice.

Now, say hello to your own physical body and yourself inside your body, which is the real you. Visualize all of the "you"s collecting up into one single *you* directly in front of your body, and bring this consolidated you into your body. Then take a magnet and run it through the spaces all the "you"s were in, collecting up the energy of all those people and tasks. Once all this space is clean, bless the magnet, hand the magnet over to God or send it out into the universe, and ask that these things be taken care of without you having to do them all yourself—unless doing them all yourself is in your own highest good. Check behind you to see if you left out any "you"s.

Remember: if you ever have the feeling you are the only one who can do what you think needs to be done, you are most likely very wrong! It may just be that help has not shown up yet, because you were afraid to let it show up.

### EXERCISE
### Calling back your energy as light

Close your eyes and turn inward. Imagine that you are a pinpoint of light within the center of your mind or your heart. Notice or choose a color for yourself as this point of light. Imagine that you as the light are a magnet, and what it's attracting is all of your own energy.

Imagine you are pulling all of yourself out of wherever you've been, from projects, people, the past, and the future. See the color coming out of these things and going to you. As it comes to you, you as the pinpoint are now getting bigger and bigger until you are a huge ball of light that is like an entire sun shining through the atmosphere of the planet of your body. Continue to call back yourself and your life force to your center until you are the enormous, shimmering being you were meant to become.

### EXERCISE
## Strengthen and enlarge your energy field with breath

Close your eyes and turn inward. Visualize your head stretching up as high as it will go, and then your feet stretching down for miles. See every part of your body expanding until you are as large as an entire city. Now see your body filling from the solar plexus with light. Let this light be plentiful and enough for your entire body.

Breathe. Play with your breath. With every inhalation of your breath, draw in more light. With every exhalation, see yourself growing even bigger in every direction. Now bring your body back to its regular dimensions, but let the light part of it stay out there.

## EXERCISE
### Everyday play

Every time you look in the mirror, imagine that you can see your spirit shining through your body. See it as much larger than your body. Play with this image throughout your day. Even if you are at the office, imagine you are so big that you become the largest thing in the room. Walk down the street imagining your spirit to be as tall as the tallest building. Feel how powerful you are as this immense energy source. Imagine that you are so big and bright that as you pass by people, they instantly shield their eyes or gasp in awe at the sight of you.

## EXERCISE
### Go back to the basics: Get those buns moving!

When you move your body, you move energy and manufacture more of it. Here's a little secret that millions of yogis figured out a long time ago: the pairing of physical and spiritual exercises (e.g., meditation, visualization) can do more for your health, mind, emotional state, appearance, and manifestation powers than either of these by themselves. Our bodies weren't meant to just sit still for long periods of time. Doing the meditations in this book while you exercise is extremely powerful! Don't exclude one in favor of the other. If you suffer from exhaustion, exercising your body may just be the thing you need more than anything else. Such exercise might require you to drag your body out of the house kicking and screaming all the way down to the gym, the pool, the track, the park, the backyard, the skating rink, the yoga or karate studio, or wherever it can move freely. You can do it!

> Not what we have, but what we enjoy,
> constitutes our abundance.
> —JOHN PETIT-SENN

# 8

# YOU CAN HAVE IT ALL!

## Faulty assumptions

Many people think they have to sacrifice one goal for another. This is just not true! Our goals seem to compete with each other not because of the goals themselves, but because of faulty assumptions about the goals or because of some limitation within ourselves. If we need a job and want to be happy but are convinced jobs can only bring us misery, then we will either create a miserable job or remain unemployed, which may bring us more stress than joy.

I have a client who watched his father work two jobs until he died of cancer. This client sincerely believes jobs are evil and has never been able to hold one for very long. Instead, he has chosen to work for himself. Yet his self-employment has required him to work much longer hours than he would have with a nine-to-five job. He has no organizational or money-management skills, and it's clear he has had to undergo much more stress than he would if he were working for someone else. His life has turned out like his father's, full of stress! This is because his father's problems had nothing to do with holding a job; they had to do with his own workaholic tendencies and poor coping skills that he passed down to his son. When we completely close ourselves to a particular option in search of freedom, we are really doing the opposite—restricting our freedom.

## Competing goals and competing parts

A frequent image that appears to me when doing clairvoyant readings is that of my client's feet going in two different directions. You can imagine how far that person would get if this were really the case! This image suggests there are oppositional forces within the client striving for different things, which is causing the client conflict or getting the client nowhere, fast. For example, one part might long for excitement, change, and a new start, while another part is demanding stability and security.

We all have these different parts to ourselves, and they have been categorized and labeled so many different things over the years. Some of these labels include: the inner child/parent/adult, the ego/id/superego, mind/body/spirit, devil/angel on the shoulder, the north/east/west/south parts of ourselves, or the shadow/light self. It really doesn't matter what we call these parts of ourselves (although some people get pretty attached to these labels). Rather, the names merely serve to help us distinguish between the different parts.

What's most important is understanding that each part or aspect has its own needs and wants. These parts take turns playing the dominant role. The part that is dominant is usually that which is in the most pain or fear, and therefore the one that is heard the loudest or has the most influence on our manifestations at any given time. When we can accept and recognize these different parts of ourselves, we begin to learn how to work with them and eventually choose which part will win the role of leadership. This is called "being conscious."

Some people are unable to observe and assess themselves. They actually become the part that is in the most fear. When we become this part, we are filled with the pain of that part and we lose perspective of the larger picture of our lives and ourselves. This is called "being unconscious." In his book *A New Earth*, Eckhart Tolle labels this the "fear body."

Some people are aware of these parts—but rather than befriend them, they exile them. The problem is that these parts never comply, they just go further undercover. This happens frequently with spiritually oriented people who are trying to become a picture of perfection (i.e., ascend). Unfortunately, trying to suppress or ignore these parts is about as effective as throwing a blanket over a monkey and pretending it's not there.

### To move or not to move

People often struggle with the question of whether or not to relocate to a new area. This struggle has to do with the various parts of themselves (and others). For simplicity's sake, let's say you are single and feeling like you really need a change. You haven't been feeling very fulfilled lately, and it seems as though your current city or town has a dead feeling to it. You'd like to move somewhere with more opportunities for employment, and where you can meet some interesting, spiritually oriented people.

Let's say you've actually been considering moving for a few years. However, another part of you is comfortable with your routine. It likes the familiarity of your current location. Sure, life is boring, but it's easy, and this part of you doesn't want the upset, the risks, the turmoil. You could call this part of you "the one that is in fear," and then disregard this fear because we've been taught that fear is bad. However, this isn't really going to help, any more than it helps to tell a terrified child who thinks he's just seen a ghost under his bed not to be afraid. The fact is, there are going to be new things to contend with if you move. Ghosts can be real or imaginary.

If you just try to ignore the fear and the fear is quite strong, then you will fail to find the right place to live, or you will manifest circumstances in life that will make it even more difficult to move. However, if you are conscious of this fear, you can befriend it and become its counselor. You can come to a compromise, promising it that if you do move, you are going to find a place where it will end up feeling safer than ever before.

**Solution: Talking to your fear**

Once you become aware of a part of yourself that is fearful and perhaps blocking the other part or parts of you that long for a change, begin a dialog with that fear. I advise you to get out a sheet of paper and divide it into half. On one half of the paper, invite the fear to write down all of its concerns all at once. Then you can you can go back through the list, and on the other half of the paper, write down the opposites of these concerns, which will be the most pleasant outcomes imaginable. Hold on to a vision of each desired outcome in your mind's eye before moving on to the next concern.

Repeat the process until all of your concerns have been addressed. Ground yourself. Next, cut the paper in two and tear up into tiny pieces the half with your fears, which you can burn or flush down the toilet. Take the half of the paper with the desired outcomes and hang it over your bed, looking often at your desired outcomes. Wait and see what gifts arrive in your life!

## Our contradictory desires can sometimes really get the best of us!

I recently attended a training in San Diego that utilized some pretty forceful energies for healing and transformation. My friend RayNelle Williams, a powerful and enthusiastic healer, decided to go, too, and we made plans to share a hotel room. RayNelle had asked me to carpool with her, as San Diego is about 160 miles from our area, but I had some reservations about not having my own car with me. I struggled for two weeks with the decision of whether to go with her or drive myself. I finally told RayNelle I'd drive alone, but the morning of our trip I called her at nine o'clock to tell her I'd changed my mind. However, she informed me she was already one third of the way there, and that she planned to get to the hotel by 3:00 PM, so she could relax. I was disappointed, but I thought, *Well, it's my own darn fault.*

Once I got on the road I hit terrible traffic. I filled up the gas tank and stopped at an outlet mall to pass some time, but when I got back on the freeway the traffic was even worse. I noticed I was still seventy miles from San Diego; I couldn't imagine driving the rest of the way, bored and alone in the awful traffic.

Suddenly my Mercedes slowed down and then completely stopped in the far-left lane of the freeway. I floored the gas pedal, but it didn't move. The engine continued to purr as it usually did, and not a single warning light came on. I gave the car gas, yelling at it, "You can't stop here on the freeway!" which prompted the car to move enough so I could inch over to the next lane and then the next, until I finally made it to the shoulder, at which point the car completely stopped again.

I thought of calling RayNelle for help, but I noticed it was already 3:30, and I thought, *She must already be at the hotel, probably in the hot tub by now. I couldn't ask her to come all this way and get me.* So I shut off the engine and waited. When I turned on the engine again, the car started back up and this time moved full speed ahead.

Reluctant to risk repeating this scenario, I drove to a strip mall next to the freeway and had another thought of calling RayNelle. *Oh, what the heck, I'll just tell her I'm going to be pretty late*, I decided. However, when I called her, she wasn't at the hotel. It turned out RayNelle was only four miles ahead of me on the same freeway, and so she doubled back and picked me up. We soon realized that if she was four miles ahead in this traffic at the time I called her, she must have been practically in the same spot I was when my car came to a complete stop. It is very possible that if I had looked around, she might have been right next to me.

I had my car towed home (thank you, Triple A!). Meanwhile, RayNelle and I had a terrific drive together to San Diego.

Some people might say this story is a coincidence; I say it was the work of my inner genie in combination with RayNelle's. Since she and I were already engaging in some strong energetic fields associated with the workshop, our desires were even more magnified. Fortunately, I set the intention a long time ago that if my car ever broke down, it would always be an easy, even pleasant experience getting my car and myself to where we needed to go. I suggest you set the same intention.

### EXERCISE
### Synchronizing your goals

Go inward, take a few deep breaths, and center yourself behind your third eye. Visualize a triangle or pyramid. Give this triangle or pyramid a grounding cord that runs deep into the earth. Imagine that you are drawing a circle or bubble at each point. (You can also see this as a rose or other three-dimensional object.) Inside each bubble, write the name of a goal. The goal could be related to money, work, spirituality, relationships, school, and so on. It could also encompass qualities such as peace, joy, passion, and amusement. Once you have done this visualization, you can imagine you are dropping the name of one of your goals into one of the bubbles (it doesn't matter which one).

Next, ask for a color to appear that represents each goal and allow it to appear or fill up the corresponding bubble. Once you have three colors, move your attention to the sides of the triangle that connect the three goal bubbles. Notice whether or not each side is in alignment, or straight or unbroken, or if one is harder to see or damaged in any way. This will be indicative of trouble between your goals.

### Heal your triangle

Next, imagine that the sides of the triangle are columns of light connecting each goal. What you want to do here is to clear out the columns (which represent the relationships between each one) and create a unifying energy field between each one. To do this, imagine that you have a very sticky ball that will easily suck up any unwanted energy or resistance. Begin to circulate this ball through the lines of the triangle and through each bubble as well. Imagine that this ball is acting as a vacuum cleaner.

Run this through the triangle several times. Then you can choose a unifying color, and see this color running through each side of the triangle and each bubble until the entire triangle is glowing with this color. Know as you do this that you are aligning and activating your goals.

Then simply go about your life for the next few days and observe what happens. You may be surprised that certain conflicts disappear, that your confusion lifts, or previously challenging decisions become quite obvious.

If someone you love hurts you, cry a river,
build a bridge, and get over it.
—AUTHOR UNKNOWN

9

# fREEING YOURSELf fROM
# PAST CREATIONS

## The power to destroy

When attempting to manifest any desire, you must
make sure you are prepared for it to come in. This
means you need to have enough time, space, and
energy for it. By taking physical action to prepare for
it, you are demonstrating a commitment to your goal,
and sending out a stronger signal than if you merely
thought about it. Often what is required is to let go of
that which no longer serves you.

If you'd like to have a baby, then cutting back on your work hours, relocating from a studio apartment to a place with an extra bedroom, and perhaps even purchasing some books on child rearing would all be good ideas. If you'd like to manifest a job or business that is really important to you, it may be easier to do so by extracting yourself from your current one. If you'd like to create a healthy new relationship, you need to let go of energetic attachments to former ones. Doing so may require you to clean your home of belongings that you shared, and will definitely require that you let go of your emotional and energetic attachments to your ex. I understand this is easier said than done! However, I have done readings on many people who were having trouble manifesting a new relationship, and an energetic attachment to an ex was usually a very large part of the problem, even if the two people had been separated for years.

*Destroy* is another word for letting go. Many people don't like this word, because they think it's too violent. Destroying doesn't have to be a bad word, however. It can be quite fun and liberating. What is wrong with destroying an inanimate object that has no feelings? We have so many connotations attached to our belongings. We have a particularly hard time letting go of that which was difficult to acquire in the first place, or more expensive, or what was given to us by a person who we believe would be offended if we just gave the things up.

What need to be examined are the feelings of guilt and anxiety that arise when we look at letting go or doing what we please with any given object or relationship. When they go unexamined, these things tend to inhibit our choices and behavior. In general, I believe some boys and men have an easier time with letting go than women do. They like to build things and then break them, while we stand by in horror, fearing someone is going to get hurt, or a mess will be made, or too much time and good materials will be wasted. Part of this might be due to the fact that as women, most of us aren't too keen about building the things or fixing them in the first place. Our female energy goes toward making everyone and everything copacetic and safe. Now, that being said, please understand I am not at all suggesting that multitudes of men don't also have a hard time letting go—all you have to do is look in the garage, or in the newspaper.

Most people don't see letting go or the ability to destroy as a skill or asset, but think about it: if you can't get rid of the things you don't need, there won't be room for your new creations. Or you will be afraid to create new things out of fear you might have to put up with them for the rest of your life, whether or not you are enjoying them. We've probably all known a packrat, or at least seen one on *Oprah* or *Dr. Phil*.

These people have collected so much junk in their homes, there is hardly any room for themselves. They can barely function, if at all.

Some people who are seriously mentally ill also have this problem. They live in clutter, garbage, and filth. This is because these people are as cluttered on the inside as they are on the outside. Others put up a good appearance on the outside, but on the inside they are stuffed too full with the energy of everyone they've ever known. They cannot possibly be present with anyone they meet, because a part of them is engaged in a million conversations and judgments and pain pictures. If any of this is describing you, then you need to improve your ability to destroy.

### EXERCISE
### Target practice

Close your eyes, take a few deep breaths. Visualize an object that you like: this could be a flower, a piece of fruit, a letter, a number, even SpongeBob SquarePants. Observe its color, shape, size, and texture. Then say goodbye to it and destroy it. Imagine you are putting a bomb under it, and watch it explode or disintegrate. Then if there are any remaining pieces, roll these up into a ball and repeat this exercise until they are gone. Once you are done, either re-create the same object or choose a new object to create and destroy.

## Destroy something for real

First, ground yourself. Then go find a few objects in your house that no longer bring you joy. Now get a hammer and smash them to pieces. Notice what emotions come up for you here.

## Clean out your house!

Your next task also involves physical action. Go ahead and get rid of whatever you can part with. Go clean out your closets and drawers. Notice what comes up for you as you do this. Items to target: Anything you haven't worn or used in the last two years. Knick-knacks that you never really liked in the first place or that have more than a coating of dust on them. Books or class notes you will never have a reason to read, and any bills that aren't current. Try donating some of these things and throwing some away, and stay conscious during the process of how it feels to part with your things.

When you encounter indecision, memories, or anxiety, don't let your feelings or emotions stop you from taking action—just be aware of them. Notice that the harder it was to obtain these things, the harder it is to let them go. Notice if you have a harder time letting go of items that were gifts versus those that you purchased yourself. Notice if you've been keeping things

you didn't need or even like because you were concerned about how someone else might feel if you gave
them up. Notice if these things have been creating
more stress for you—and more work, time, or energy
than if you'd never had them in the first place.

Regardless of how expensive it was, how hard it
was to obtain, whom it was from, where you got it, or
where it's going, if it's taking up space in your dwelling,
your garage, or your mind, then why on earth should
you remain shackled to it? If you are worried you might
change your mind in the future, then let go of this
worry and trust that you will be able to find what you
need again or something better the next time around.
Trust in your ability to create and re-create.

### Suggestions for letting go

Invite your friends over to help you choose what to let
go of. Have a yard sale and make arrangements prior
to the sale for where you will bring the remaining
items that don't sell. Host a destroying party! Build
a big bonfire (call the fire department first to ensure
this is permissible in your area) and invite all your
friends to bring either objects they want to burn in the
fire or symbols of objects/relationship/situations they
are seeking to let go of. Make this a gourmet potluck
party, so after you are done destroying you can have a
gluttonous celebration. A soak in a hot tub at the end
of the night will seal the deal on the new you.

**Are your past creations now haunting you?**
A few years ago I began to notice something rather odd. Some of the things I had been attempting to manifest three to six years ago, into which I had put huge amounts of energy, were beginning to show up in my life. Rather than being happy about this, however, it was proving to be quite annoying! These relationships or things were no longer in alignment with who I was. I didn't want these things or people anymore, but they were hell-bent on having me! Their presence or manifestation was making it difficult for me to move forward. I found that the same amount of effort and struggle I had put into them years before was now being required in order to get rid of them.

I've seen this happen with other conscious creators as well. When it does happen, it's important to understand how we are not obligated to accept these things or people; we can send them back.

### EXERCISE
### Bringing our creations into present time
Go inward. Ground and center yourself behind your third eye. Visualize a timeline out in front of you, running from left to right. This timeline can have negative numbers representing the past and positive numbers representing the future, with the 0 directly in front of you.

First, focus on yourself at the zero point. Remind yourself that your body is always in the present moment; it cannot exist in the past or future, only your mind can. Then begin to align your mind with the zero point. Your body is in the present, but your spirit might be trapped somewhere else. Call your energy back from the future or from the past to the zero point.

Next, create a clear, transparent rose and place it at the zero point. Inside it see a symbol representing that which you wish to create. Call all of your energy into this rose with the symbol. Let the rose show you the color of joy that will emanate from you when this symbol manifests into physical reality. Then see the rose growing bigger and bigger until it covers the entire timeline.

### EXERCISE
## Ending past-time agreements

You can do this exercise on paper or in your imagination. If you are married and desiring a divorce, you can make a photocopy of your original marriage agreement and use that, or you can write up a list of the terms of what you believe made up the original agreement. These would not only include the official language (*to have and to hold, in sickness and in health*) but also what seemed to be the unspoken agreements or terms. If you never had an official agreement, or this relationship is between yourself and a sibling or friend, you can just write up a list of what you contributed in the relationship and what the other person contributed.

Take a good look at this agreement, and then you can either rewrite it if you'd like to re-create the relationship on different terms, or just tear it up into little pieces if you are completely ready to let go. Ground yourself as you do this, and visualize any cords running between the two of you cut or falling away as you break the agreement. (Refer to chapter 3 if you need a reminder of how to ground yourself.) Then burn the original agreement. Just watch out: this seemingly innocuous exercise can have enormous effects that will register with the person (or people) with whom you are ending your agreements.

### The past does not dictate the future (unless you let it)!

You may have heard that phrase before, but it bears repeating. I'd even recommend using it as a mantra if you feel fear or anxiety about getting back into a new relationship after ending a traumatic one, or going back into a certain line of work that didn't appeal to you when you were in it years ago.

*It is absolutely essential that you realize you can re-create your life over and over again in new ways.* Just because you've had jobs in the past where you were surrounded by rude, uncaring, envious people does not mean your next job will be like that. Just because someone cheated on you before doesn't mean your new love will behave in the same way. Just because your business failed or you went bankrupt ten years ago does not mean your new business is doomed as well, or that you should avoid starting a new one.

As long as we are learning from our past experiences, as long as we are conscious of what led us into unpleasant situations and what helped us get out of them, we will be less likely to re-create the same situation.

In many of the readings I've done, I've seen people really forget to update their self-image in the workplace. You now know so much more than you did when you began your job. Even if you've just had a career change, you are so much wiser than you were when you first entered the workplace. You are deserving of an easier day, of more assistance, of more respect, of more freedom and time to take care of yourself. If your job, boss, and co-workers are not reflecting this back to you, then as long as you are in this particular environment, you are not believing in the facts about what you deserve and you are not standing up for yourself. The idea that you must be a workhorse and just "take it" in order to get a paycheck may very well have been part of your past or your parents' truth, but it does not have to be yours. There are alternatives, even for the likes of you!

If you know what I'm talking about here, and you decide to change jobs or careers but again find yourself right back in a similar situation, this is evidence that you have some inner work to do. Usually, as we move from a place of endurance to a place of respecting and expecting better for ourselves in present time, we find ourselves having a bit more of what we wish for in each job or position, until finally we wake up one day to discover we are looking forward to going to work, that we love our bosses, and that our bosses love us. Often this is because we have become our own boss!

EXERCISE

**Mantra**

Repeat one hundred times, at least three times a day: *I am worthy of absolute respect by right of my presence as a living, breathing being, and I will remain true to myself even in the presence of those who have not yet learned this fact.*

EXERCISE

**Healing your past creations**

Relax and go inward. Instruct yourself to allow the most unpleasant memories of your last job or relationship to come up. This might be a bit painful, but spend just a minute or so letting each memory come up. Don't dwell for more than twenty seconds on each one. Then visualize a garbage can or pit with huge flames shooting out of it. Imagine you are dropping all those memories right into the flames and they are being burned up. Once they are all gone, the flames will extinguish themselves. You can then imagine you are taking the remaining ash and burying it deep in the center of the earth, or dumping it in the middle of the sea, where the ashes will disintegrate and the tiniest pieces will be eaten by colorful fish.

Once you have done the above, imagine yourself at work or in a relationship having the opposite of what you had before. If you had a rude, demanding boss, see a sweet, angelic-looking manager handing you more awards of achievement than you can find space for on your wall. If you had a boyfriend who rarely called or was miserable all the time, see a new man all smiles, who can't stop hugging you and is the warmest, happiest person in the world. Visualize these people often, and even have conversations with them as you are cleaning your house or driving to work. Make them your imaginary friends, pretend they are your imaginary soul mates. Listen to them as they speak back to you with encouragement and grace. The more fun you have with this exercise, the more easily you will manifest their counterparts on the physical plane. Most importantly, do not just expect that there will be positive change. *Demand* it. Scream out loud to the universe that it will be there for you and you there for it.

When one door of happiness closes, another opens;
but often we look so long at the closed door
that we do not see the one which has been opened for us.
—HELEN KELLER

10

# HAVINGNESS VS. LIMITS—
# HOW HIGH CAN YOU GO?

In every area of our lives, including relationships, money, and freedom, we develop and operate from conscious and unconscious parameters as to what we believe is possible or not possible for ourselves. These parameters can also be considered "limits." These limits may be quite low in one area and quite high in another. Our limits are part of a belief system of which we are only partially conscious. They have been influenced by our past experiences and those of our ancestors. These limits are sometimes other people's projections in the form of judgment, doubt, and blame. The "limit" is whatever line is drawn at the top of this threshold that says, "Stop! It's not possible or safe to go beyond this point." These limits are intricately connected to our self-esteem.

Our limits of what we can allow ourselves to have are often set at the same levels as our parents' limits. If we are ready on a soul level to exceed these limits, then we may encounter our parents' resistance on an energy level (if our parents are deceased or unaware of what we are doing) or on the physical level, as when they try to tell us that what we are doing is not possible or is dangerous or is selfish or why it just won't work. If we demonstrate that it is possible for us, then they can no longer hold on to the belief that it was or is truly impossible for them. Many people go to great lengths to protect themselves from this truth. So your success could be very threatening to your parents. Or it can inspire them, which it often will.

One of the first things a clairvoyant might see when reading a person who is coming up against these limits is an image of a wall or a ceiling. Then the clairvoyant's task is to see what the wall or ceiling represents, what is needed to break it down, how strong or high it really is, and what is on the other side. By getting a glimpse of what is on the other side, the clairvoyant sees the life the client is longing to have.

## How much is enough?

The term *havingness* can be defined as the extent to which people allow themselves to have something good and important. This term emerged from spiritualists and clairvoyants, who noticed that a person's ability to manifest good things in his or her life is intricately linked with how much that person feels he or she deserves these things, as well as the person's underlying belief system about how much of something it is really possible to have.

Most of the time, lower havingness shows itself in the extent of what we can have, rather than whether or not we can have it. Someone may feel that he can have a relationship but not one that completely fulfills him. Someone may feel that she can have a high-paying job but not one that she can enjoy. Someone else might believe that adults are not supposed to have too much fun, laugh too much, or change much once they reach a certain age. I remember hearing my father saying more than once, "Most of life is about struggle. You can only hope to have a few scattered moments of happiness, but the majority of life is boring and mundane." Even at an early age I knew he was speaking from a place of depression and a limited belief system, and this was not a universal truth, even if there were and are numerous others who believe the same thing.

I think some of these limits come from a real need to stay in balance. For example, most people can't eat everything they desire without feeling sick or gaining too much weight. We know what happens when we totally overdo it. We do need boundaries and standards in order to function as healthy human beings. However, we begin to have problems and experience the "stuckness" when these boundaries or standards become so solidified that they rule us rather than the other way around. This happens when we lose awareness of them, or when we never had awareness of them to begin with. Fortunately, the moment we become aware of these limits, they begin to shift.

## Allow yourself to have even more than you already have!

Last year I attended a workshop held by Michael J. Tamura, the author of *You Are the Answer: Discovering and Fulfilling Your Soul's Purpose*, and his wife, Raphaelle, a woman who has mastered the art of being loving and compassionate while speaking her mind. The workshop was pricey, but I justified the cost by telling myself this would be a great opportunity to visit with some friends I hadn't seen in a number of years who live in the area.

Around the third day of the workshop, I began feeling a bit stressed out about the long drive back home and how I would squeeze in time to see my friends. I went up to Raphaelle and advised her that I was not going to be there for the final morning, since I felt I needed to start heading back. She told me outright she thought this was a terrible idea. "I think you're hitting a limit of how much you can allow yourself to have all you are getting from this workshop," she advised me.

"But I've already gotten so much from it," I countered, which was true. One of the reasons I was fine or almost fine with leaving was because I really felt that I had already gotten my money's worth. If I left now, I could fit in meetings with a few friends.

"Yes, you have already gotten a lot," Raphaelle responded. "But there's the limit. Why can't you allow yourself to have even more? Why can't you find a way to stay and see your friends, and have your return trip be stress-free, even fun? You're a creative person. I'm sure you can do this."

Raphaelle had her mind made up even if I didn't. I told her I'd think about it, and crawled back to my seat with my tail between my legs, not sure if what she was saying was true or if she just didn't understand my predicament. However, half out of guilt, half out of a fear she might be right, I decided to stay. The next day we did some of the most powerful meditations I had done in the past ten years. I also received an awesome healing from my instructor. These things propelled me into a higher vibrational state than I had consciously experienced in years, and I made some major changes in my life after that.

At the end of the workshop I called the friend of mine I was most excited to see. It turned out she was visiting another mutual friend in a town directly on my way home. I arrived there just in time to have a wonderful dinner with both of them. The rest of my ride was relaxing, and easier than I had ever imagined. I didn't even get sleepy, which I usually do. This experience confirmed for me what havingness really means. It means having more than we think we can have or than we allow ourselves to have. This experience also reminded me to strive always for more, just in case there is more to be had—even when I think I am getting something terrific. This doesn't negate being appreciative for every tiny thing I do have, but just reminds me to be open to the possibility of even more: more love, more wonder, more passion, more abundance. I've discovered that just when we think we've found all there is to find, there is even more for the taking, or having.

The ability to have more absolutely requires one to ask for more—more from oneself, more from others, and more from the universe/God/whatever guiding force is out there. Many people find that once they do manage to manifest more than they had before, it's easy to stop there. If paying your rent or mortgage was an issue, once you have that under control there may not seem to be as much incentive to continue to manifest money or put as much energy into that goal. But wouldn't it be nice to be able to pay rent *and* take a vacation when you want one, or have enough money to take a class or workshop whenever you come across one that piques your interest?

I was thinking just this morning about how much I love so many of my clairvoyant students, particularly the ones I work with individually. I began thinking, *How is it possible that there are really this many wonderful, talented people in my life that have as much passion for these subjects as I do?* It was really so hard for me to believe, even though there's no denying they are present in my life! I think I just went for so many years without meeting lots of people like this, that it still seems surreal. Then I thought, *Well, I'm likely to meet and be surrounded by a whole lot more of these beautiful souls. What on earth will that be like!* Can I really let myself have that?

### Manifesting

The following technique is one of the most powerful you can use for manifesting any goal. It doesn't matter how much you want something or how many hours you spend visualizing it and affirming it. If you can't really let yourself have it, for whatever reason, you aren't ever going to see it. This exercise will both let you know how much of something you can have, and will let you release or get rid of the limits I've discussed. This technique has been taught to me by several different teachers, and I've modified it slightly based on my own personal preferences.

## Creating and working with a havingness gauge

Close your eyes and ground yourself. Visualize an enormous movie theater-type screen in front of you. Imagine there is a huge transparent bubble out in front of you. Write the name of the thing you'd like to have for yourself above the bubble. Drop your named request (e.g., more love, more romance, more money, more fun) in the bubble and ask for the bubble to fill up with the energy of that which you'd like to create. Inside the bubble, see an image of yourself receiving this thing or quality and experiencing it. See yourself looking gleeful, and then feel as much happiness as you can muster. Come on, you can still pretend, even if you think you're all grown up! After you've basked in the joy of your success, give this bubble a very strong and heavy grounding cord.

Next to the bubble, visualize an enormous gauge. You can see this gauge however you'd like. Many people like to see it going from 1 to 100, but you don't have to restrict yourself to that. Ask yourself how much "havingness" you currently have for the thing or vibration you'd like to manifest for yourself. Watch the gauge and notice where the arrow goes. Make a mental note of what happens.

If the gauge is at any less than 100, or even if it's at 100 or exceeds your top setting, imagine you are taking one of your fingers, or pressing a lever, and increasing the number on the gauge to the highest level you are comfortable with at this moment. As you raise the gauge, refocus on your bubble's grounding cord and tell it to release whatever energy has been getting in the way of you having this goal for yourself. You may want to imagine you are fastening or securing the gauge at this higher setting with some kind of apparatus that holds it in place, like a rubber band. Next, return your attention back to your bubble beside the gauge and watch to see what new colors come out and down the grounding cord. You might see some images of symbols or even people you know.

Once you feel your bubble is clear, drop the gauge with its new setting into your bubble and watch what happens to it. Then fill it with the brightest light you can imagine. This is the light of spirit, where everything is possible and there are no limits. Watch this light for as long as you'd like. Then you can either cut the cord and let it float off into the universe to start manifesting for you, or see it going up to the light or to the hands of God.

Don't be concerned if, when doing this exercise, you start to get spacey, forget what you are doing, or

feel some kind of pain. There is a lot of unconscious-
ness involved in our permission to have, and what this
exercise is doing is reprogramming your unconscious
mind. In fact, every time I tried to write about this
exercise, I got so incredibly exhausted that I had to go
lie down; that's because I'm working through my own
limits when I write about this experience.

You don't need to use only a bubble for this exercise. Sometimes working with more intricate objects
can be even more powerful. For example, you can use
an image of a flower instead of a bubble, and then
watch what happens to the flower as you work with
the energy. You can also use any geometrical shape of
your choice, and then watch how it transforms after
working with the gauge.

### Your ability to give and receive must be in balance

People often restrict themselves in the *way* a goal can
manifest. They can only allow themselves to have or
receive money if they've earned it themselves. Some
people not only have to earn the money themselves,
but also believe earning it can or will only come from
hard work. This places quite a limit on their prosperity, since there are only so many hours in one day that
a person can work. These people often look at others
who aren't working as hard or who don't have to
work at all for their money with a mixture of envy

or resentment, tinged with an underlying feeling of hopelessness.

Many people really hold the picture, through their thoughts and accompanying emotions, that there is something wrong with accepting gifts, charity, or even emotional support. Some people have an exaggerated sense of fairness. They believe that whatever they receive must be equally reciprocated, and vice versa, so they will neither ask for nor accept help unless they feel they have something of equal value to give in return.

A man from Texas I once dated is one of the most extreme examples that I have ever encountered of someone who cannot receive. One day a bunch of his friends threw a birthday party for him at a ritzy restaurant. Each of the individual's tabs was no less than eighty dollars, but this wouldn't have made a dent in most of their designer wallets. However, my friend excused himself during the dinner and went and paid the entire bill, which totaled close to two thousand dollars, before his friends could have a chance to pay themselves. When his friends found out what he had done, many of them were visibly distressed. A couple of them were outright furious. They had looked at this occasion as an opportunity to treat him to dinner, something he apparently rarely allowed (although he had confided to me more than once that he feared many women were out to get his money). What had been a really fun event ended on a sour note. And the story doesn't end there.

We arrived back at his place, and it took quite a while to carry in all the beautifully wrapped gifts his friends had surprised him with. When he turned off the lights and climbed into bed, I couldn't believe he could possibly even think about sleeping before opening his gifts, but that's exactly what he did! I was up at the crack of dawn as if it were Christmas. However, he slept in. Before work he made time for breakfast, e-mails, and a scan of the morning paper, but he insisted his presents were going to have to wait. (Arggghh!)

Days, then weeks, then a month went by, and the presents were still sitting there in the corner of the living room, the ribbons' shine dimmed with the dust of time. Now when I looked at them, my curiosity as to what was inside the boxes had turned almost to a desperation to understand why someone wouldn't want to open a bunch of presents. My pleading with him to open his gifts became such a point of contention between us that I knew if I kept pressing the issue, it would be the end of our relationship.

One day I stopped in to say hi on my way to an interview in his neighborhood, and I asked him if I could borrow an umbrella. He was absorbed in his reading and mumbled something about the hall closet. I wasn't sure which closet he was referring to, so I opened the one nearest to me and had one of the biggest shocks of my life. The large closet was jam-packed, from the floor to the very top shelf, with unopened, dusty, wrapped presents. Hundreds of them. By the looks of it, these gifts must have been piling up in that closet for years.

I looked over at my friend and felt such sadness. Some of it was for all those people who had gone out of their way to get him something they thought he'd enjoy, but most of it was for him and the inner starvation his very soul must surely suffer from.

Sometime later he revealed to me that throughout his childhood, his father, who was an oil-company executive, would not allow him to keep gifts that other people had given him during holidays and on his birthday.

While this is obviously an extreme example, think back to your own life. How many times has someone offered to pay for lunch, or done something to make your life a little easier, and you either outright refused or engaged in a silly back-and-forth argument until you were satisfied that you had objected long enough to retain your dignity and honor? In many cultures, this silliness is expected.

### We all are deserving of help

Like a welfare office, we all maintain a list of the types of people who we feel deserve extra help. Those on our lists include the helpless, such as the very young, the old, and the ill or abused. Women used to be in this category but with the "success" of the women's movement, they were bumped right off of it. Anyone else who needs help is instead handed judgment. This could include our own children, who may have grown older than the maximum age requirement of the list.

People can find themselves in a position where they cannot take care of themselves and must rely on the charity of others, because an aspect of their soul is helping them learn how to receive. Their body and overall happiness may have been sacrificed because of an unconscious desire or need to be absolutely self-sufficient at all times. Such people hold not only themselves to this standard, but also everyone else around them. Those who aren't aware of this end up feeling overwhelmed and unsupported, because such people tend to attract others who rely on them instead of nurture them.

**We never truly see the whole picture**
I think we all need to be very careful about making our own assumptions about who really is in need. We must stop judging those who we think shouldn't be in that position. Even when we live with someone, we do not necessarily understand all of what that person is going through, what pressures that person is dealing with, or what he or she is trying to or is meant to achieve.

My siblings who do not yet have children of their own sometimes get irritated with me because I ask more of them than they do of me right now. About once a month, when my significant other is not available, I will ask them to watch my son for a day or even a few days when I have to go out of town to teach. Of course Manny is thrilled to spend time with his aunts and uncles. However, this means that my siblings have to adjust their schedules or drive out of their way to get him or meet me somewhere. Sometimes (okay, usually most of the time) I am doing so many things at once that I arrive late, miss some family functions, or decide to leave these functions early. Then my siblings get mad at me.

Being psychic, I can tell the exact moment when they're holding a complaint session on my behalf, which is usually confirmed later. I am not sure if it's the offense itself of being tardy or absent, or the fact that I don't profusely express guilt and remorse that bothers them more. I no longer believe in allowing myself to be punished by negative emotions for upsetting others, and so I push aside the guilt. I feel that if a family member is upset that I have to leave her party early to go home and do something that will pay my bills, then she has other options than to choose to get angry at me. She can send me supportive thoughts of love, or she can offer to help pay my bills!

I sometimes find myself defending my behavior and attitude by reminding myself I have worked long and hard to allow myself to ask for help when I need it. I tell myself my siblings are benefiting because they get the pleasure of hanging out with my son. Also, this doesn't come close to the energy, time, and effort I am expending in helping others. My siblings don't make this connection, so to them I am just thinking of myself, which I understand. They actually have no idea what I am doing on an energy level for them, but that's okay, too. Sometimes I do tell them that if they just offered to help more, they wouldn't feel as though I was always asking.

Now, if you are as perceptive as I think you are, you are going to notice that I am using the fact that I help a lot of people to justify asking for help myself. You will recall that I said I've learned how to push aside guilt, but the truth is that we can only push aside what is still there. So somewhere within me, I must believe that I am only worthy of receiving help if I am helping others—lots of others, probably way too many of them.

In the past I didn't ask for help at all so I certainly have made progress, but if I really, truly believed I was worthy of receiving for no other reason than that I exist, then my current situation would look much different. In this case I would probably have people sending me presents or checks and knocking on my door saying, "Wow! I know you are doing so much. Can I come over and cook for you, clean your house, or take Manny out for an afternoon so you can finish the third book you've written while running your own business, before you pull out every hair in that throbbing, exhausted, matted head of yours?!"

Hmmm, excuse me for a minute, I need to go check my havingness gauge!

**Can you receive in health as well as in sickness?**
My father had liver cancer last year. While my other relatives have pitied him, I've watched how he has been receiving more attention, more comfort, and more communication than he ever has in his life, not only from his extended family but also from countless medical professionals and complete strangers. He has also stopped working for the first time in about forty-five years.

While it is very unfortunate he had to go through pain (caused by his treatment as opposed to the cancer itself), he seems to be happier than I've seen him in a long time, perhaps ever. This is obviously not the experience of everyone who becomes ill, but I've seen plenty of times how illness can serve our other goals. It gives us the long-needed break we weren't allowing ourselves to have. It forces us into a position where we have to allow others to help us. It forces us to give up our need for control. Of course, the more resistant we are to being in these more vulnerable positions, the more we will kick and scream and suffer.

## Martyrs: Gotta love 'em!

There are also people who will never allow themselves to be in a position of perceived weakness. They feel it is shameful or beneath them to ask for help or love directly, and yet they are absolutely desperate for help and love. So they ask for help in a million other ways, by complaining or "silently" suffering so loudly you can't help but cut your veins and let them drink. However, when you offer them help, they will either refuse it or ignore the advice that would alleviate the suffering.

This is actually one of the strongest forms of manipulation and abuse one person can inflict on another. These people don't want to help themselves; they want you to sympathize with them and agree with the impossibility of their predicament of the month. We have all known people like this. Just look at the person in your office who has never taken a day off in twenty years, and returns the day after surgery for carpal tunnel syndrome because "someone has to type all these reports."

**We need to be able to accept
lots of help to be successful!**

There is a reason the Bible mentions so many times the acts of giving and receiving. These are abilities that really impact the quality of our lives every moment of our day. Our permission for both giving and receiving is very much determined by the norms and customs of the society we live in. When we don't allow ourselves to give or receive unconditionally, we are putting up a wall in our heart. We push away people who want to express their love through giving. When we give from our heart without expectations, whether that gift is a compliment, a kiss, a look of approval, a bouquet of flowers, or $500,000, we are affirming our aliveness and our natural abundance.

If you look at the richest, most successful people in the world, you will find individuals who have received an enormous amount of help from others. This help came from gifts, inheritances, loans, donations, and/or the dedicated commitment of employees, family, and friends. There is not a single politician in America who could have won his or her position without an enormous amount of assistance and support. There is not a single actor who has won an Oscar, or a single musician who has won a Grammy, who wasn't backed up by the support, creative talent, and genius of dozens if not hundreds of people. A break (as in the expression *the actor's big break*) is always an opportunity given to us by someone else.

## Receiving gauge

Repeat the exercise earlier in this chapter for creating a havingness gauge, but this time label your gauge as a *receiving gauge*. Let your bubble represent not only money but also the ability to receive love, nurturing, sexual gratification, attention, guidance, and so on. Your bubble could also represent receptivity as a whole in order to cover all these areas.

EXERCISE
## Direct practice

1. Make it your goal that you are going to allow yourself to receive ten things this month without saying anything other than "Thank you." That which you receive could include a compliment, help, a gift, or charity.

2. Do something for someone else once a day for an entire month. Ask and expect nothing in return, but if the other person later reciprocates, then generously accept.

3. Find five things you can delegate to other people, and then do just that.

## Discover your feelings about giving

Divide a sheet of paper into two columns. In the first column, make a list of everything you've done for other people in the last month or two. Next, with as little analyzing as possible, very quickly write down how you feel about what you did. You can simply write words such as *positive, good, happy, resentful, guilty,* and so on. Many people give with underlying agendas, strings attached, or ideas of how the other person is supposed to respond.

If you find that you felt anything less than joy in giving, that is a sign you may be giving too much of yourself, or that you may be giving from a place of fear rather than love.

### No strings attached

Many years ago I gave five dollars to a disheveled beggar who was perched outside a convenience store, mumbling to himself. I then followed him into the store to get a snack for myself, and I was shocked and angered to see him buying beer and cigarettes. I turned to him and scolded him, "I gave you that money for food, not for beer!"

His response: "But I already ate!"

As I exited the store he was back in his spot, and another woman was handing him money. Probably appearing as crazed as the mumbling beggar did, I

lunged for the cash as it was exchanging hands, trying to save the woman from making the same grievous
"mistake" I had just made.

Startled, the woman turned to me and asked
what was wrong. Out of breath, I gasped, "He's just
going to use your money on beer and cigarettes," and I
explained what I had observed.

To my surprise, the woman scolded me outright.
"Look at him. He's got to be miserable. If beer and cigarettes make his life a little easier, then I am honored
to have brought him some joy. What he does with a
gift is just none of my business."

I will never know that woman's name, but she was
one of my most important teachers.

The surest defense against evil is extreme individualism,
originality of thinking, whimsicality, even—if you will—eccentricity.
That is, something that can't be feigned, faked, imitated;
something even a seasoned imposter couldn't be happy with.
—JOSEPH BRODSKY

I I

# MANIFESTING SPACE, MONEY, RELATIONSHIPS, AND CREATIVE PROJECTS

### Making it real to the body

One of the greatest difficulties people have with creating and holding on to positive mental pictures
is that these pictures often seem to be in such stark
contrast to their present-time experience. Many of
us have learned that it's not enough to repeat empty
words. We must *feel* them. However, just try repeating
"I am infinitely abundant and overflowing with absolute prosperity" as you share a sixty-three-cent can of
Friskies chicken in gravy with your cat; you are likely

to end up wallowing in a pool of tears rather than in a fit of ecstasy. Maintaining a positive attitude as your cardboard box collapses on your head is going to be a challenge, no matter how uplifting the words you repeat.

Your physical body has its own needs apart from the desires of your mind and spirit, and it has its own memories. The body stores feelings of pleasure and pain. Your physical body records traumas, even apart from your mind and spirit. This is why one of the most effective therapies used to heal childhood trauma and abuse involves creating new memories through touch and other sensory input like sound and smell, and why people often require healing on a body level through modalities such as massage, yoga, or tai chi, in addition to talking about or visualizing away their problems.

In terms of manifesting, it is often helpful to place your physical body in situations where it can experience that which you are trying to manifest as real, in present time. Since you do not yet have the thing you are attempting to manifest, you have to be creative and put yourself in situations that will trick the body into believing it actually has that which you desire.

Below I will offer suggestions for manifesting particular goals, such as more space, peace, relationships, and creative projects.

## Space

We'll start with this one, because it's often necessary we have enough of this to ourselves before we can manifest other things. By *space* I mean enough physical distance between yourself and others, so you can think your own thoughts and have time to yourself. Before we can have space on the outside, we need to have it on the inside. Most people erroneously believe that in order to have space on the inside, they must have it on the outside, meaning they think they need to live in a house big enough that they can close the door and no one will bother them. In fact, it's often the other way around.

A few years ago my boyfriend and I made the decision to live temporarily in his motor home while we searched for a new place to live. Doing so would allow us to save money quickly. He was a bit wary of the idea, but I thought it would be a grand adventure. We did have some good times there, but it got old pretty fast.

During one particularly difficult week, I was feeling more stress than I had in years and knew what I needed more than anything was to find a quiet place to meditate. But where? I drove around town for over an hour, but every place was more hectic than the last. Every park was filled with screaming kids, leering landscapers, and clamoring construction workers. I drove to three different churches in town, thinking surely one of them would provide a respite for contemplative solitude. One was locked, the other was filled with cheerleading squads, and the last one was overrun with rancorous Boy Scouts.

I realized I was really close to my local post office, so I decided I might as well go and check my post-office box. I squealed into the crowded parking lot and waited ten minutes before a space opened up. I went inside. No mail, of course. Not even a damn bill! I returned to my car defeated and drained, started it up, but realized there was nowhere I wanted to go. Out of complete irritation I yelled, "Fine, then I'll just do it here!" The window was open, and a few heads turned to see if I intended to do anything interesting.

At first, sitting there in the frenetic parking lot was more than distracting, since car after car squealed to a halt just feet behind me, some even honking, with hopes I was about to relinquish my spot. However, within a few minutes I completely forgot where I was. At some point I went into a very deep trance, bordering on sleep, and when I woke up about an hour later, I was surprised to discover that despite it being four o'clock in the afternoon, the busiest time of day here, there were now only a couple of cars left in the parking lot. I felt refreshed now and headed back to the motor home.

I found a note taped to the squeaky door, stating that my family members had gone out for a movie and dinner, and would not be back for several hours. I sat down and meditated for another forty-five minutes or so, then read a book and took a delicious nap. By the time they returned home, I was happy to see them again. We moved a few days later to a much bigger place.

The truth that I am continuously shown is that our outer lives really do mirror our inner lives. If you have no space in your house, then you probably have little space for yourself in your aura. It's probably jam-packed with other people's ideas, feelings, consider-ations, opinions, and wishes. As we clear these out on the inside of us, it will be reflected on the outside of us. This change can literally happen overnight.

### EXERCISE
### Own your space for yourself

While you can do this exercise anywhere, including in your car, I suggest that you start off doing it in the place where you intend to spend the night.

First, see a huge cord of energy running from the base of your spine to deep within the center of the planet.

Next, imagine there is a giant rose filled with flaming light in the center of your room. See the light expand so it fits around the entire building. Now, visualize any excess energies releasing down the stem. Then see a stem shooting downward, connecting the blazing bud with the earth. See the stem grow bigger and bigger until it is the size of your room. You can increase the size of the rose and the stem to fit around the entire building. As you do this, know you are really taking charge of this space, making it roomier and safer for yourself.

Please note that if you live with other people and they unconsciously react to the effects of this exercise by becoming angry or even throwing you out, then chances are you did not belong there to begin with, and they are doing you a really big favor! Do not underestimate the power of these visualizations, or the ability of others to sense a shift in the field around them as a result. Even though most people won't have the slightest inkling of what's happening, they will feel a difference, and they may experience and react to the shift in various ways.

### EXERCISE

**Finding peace when you don't feel peaceful**

If you are not feeling very peaceful, I recommend you head outside and take at least a forty-five-minute walk where you can appreciate the beauty of nature. Take along your iPod and listen to the songs that inspire you the most, unless it's the sounds of nature that most inspire you. Find a ranch or someplace else where you can hang out with animals. Horses and cows are excellent for this, because they are always in the present moment. As you walk, use all of your senses to notice the enchanting things around you. Notice how the sunlight glimmers on the leaves of the trees, the color of the sky, and the feel of the ground beneath your feet. Doing this exercise will help get you into present time and run the energy of appreciation, which is very strong and helps you to attract other things you will appreciate as well. Once you are feeling peaceful, you are ready to begin saying your affirmations (e.g., "I am now filled with overwhelming peace, joy, appreciation," and so on).

### EXERCISE
### Crowning yourself with peace

You can also choose a color that represents peace or the state of being you choose, and imagine your crown is turning to this color. Then imagine that the color is flowing downward. See it fill up your head, throat, heart, stomach, sexual organs, and corresponding areas. See it flowing downward through the legs to the feet and out your grounding cord. See it flowing down your shoulders and fountaining out of your hands like colored pools of light. Imagine that you are so filled with the color of peace that it seeps from every pore of your skin, filling up the energy field around you.

## Manifesting a great place to live

The key here is to find a place in a neighborhood or on a piece of land where you would love to live, and physically go there. Once you are actually there, pretend you live there and admire the building and the grounds. Stand in the doorway if possible, and pretend you are greeting guests who can't believe what a fantastic place you managed to find: "Yes, I know this place is awesome. Can you believe it, me, little ol' me, now lives here? It was so easy to find and was so affordable!"

Repeat this several times to different people, whether real or imaginary. (So what if they really believe you or think you are nuts—you probably are.) Remain there as long as possible. If you can stay overnight there, all the better.

## Manifesting relationships
## by making them more real

Many children of divorce aren't sure if it's even possible to manifest a healthy relationship. It's therefore important for them, and perhaps for you, too, even if you aren't a child of divorce, to believe that such a relationship is possible. A good way to do this is to place yourself in close proximity to couples who are in seemingly healthy and happy relationships. Invite yourself over to such a couple's house for dinner and talk to them about their relationship. It's normal to feel envious or sad if they seem really happy. However, you can turn any of these feelings into resolve: if it's possible for them, then it is also possible for you. (It doesn't matter if they really are absolutely healthy or happy, as long as you think they are!)

If you don't know a couple who fit this description, then read books about healthy couples or watch films depicting such couples. These are somewhat hard to come by but do exist. One of my favorite movies depicting a wacky but happily married couple is *Meet the Fockers*, starring Dustin Hoffman and Barbra Streisand.

**Treat yourself like you'd like to be treated**
You may have heard a version of this saying before but it bears repeating, because it does work very well. In fact, it may be one of the most important phrases in this book. Spend at least part of every day pampering yourself and treating yourself exactly as you'd want to be treated in a relationship. Take yourself out to places you like, compliment yourself every time you look in a mirror, and do activities you want to do—not just ones you think you should do or must do. Lavish presents on yourself. The most important thing is to give yourself, your soul, and your body the attention it craves from someone else.

A fantastic thing you can do for yourself is to take a class or join some kind of specialized organization where you will find people who have similar interests as you.

After you do the above, take time to visualize and play around with the emotions you might feel if someone else was taking care of you and loving you like you take care of and love yourself. Many people make the mistake of thinking they can't love themselves until someone else loves them. These people are usually alone for a very long time, because if you don't love yourself you won't be able to handle the love of someone else. You won't feel worthy, and will end up pushing the love away or not recognizing it for what it is in the first place. I know it's a cliché, but *fake it till you make it* is the best advice I can give you. If you don't feel like you love yourself, pretend you do!

**Additional suggestions for making a future relationship real to your body:**
- Surround yourself with people who adore you! Ask them to tell you why you are so wonderful.
- Cut out the picture of a person, even a celebrity, whom you admire, and tape it to the front of a chair. Pretend this person is complimenting you. If this won't make you laugh at yourself, nothing will! Remember: laughter raises

your vibration, which then attracts others who are at this higher frequency.

- Draw or paint a picture of the characteristics of the person you wish to be, and hang this picture over your bed or put it under your pillow or on the pillow next to you. For that matter, you can go buy a doll (don't worry, it doesn't have to be a blow-up one!) and pretend it's your future mate. Talk to it, say words of gratitude to it, and then fall asleep hugging it. (I said *hugging* it! Come on, clean up that mind of yours!)

- Please note: I am not suggesting that you visualize yourself with the exact person you think you want to be with. If there is someone you have in mind, that person may or may not be able to fulfill your needs. Instead, visualize yourself with an imaginary person who has the characteristics that are important to you.

### Money

Many people make the mistake of thinking that the only way they can have money is to earn it. Yet often they are already feeling overwhelmed, or having difficulty figuring out how in their line of work they will ever make more than they are already earning. It is therefore often helpful to open yourself up to the idea that a windfall of money could come to you, regardless of your actions. Below I explain in more detail about the ability to have and receive money. For now it's just important to keep in mind that when you visualize money flowing to you, see it coming from sources other than, or in addition to, that which comes from your own hard labor.

EXERCISE
## Creating wealth

In order to prepare ourselves for wealth, we often need to trick ourselves into believing we already have it or are worthy of it. One way to do this is to immerse yourself in an environment where you can begin to imagine that you are compatible with the energy of wealth and to experience real physical sensations while you are visiting this environment. Here are just a few suggestions:

- Take a friend along with you who gets what you are doing. Get dressed up and spend the day visiting expensive boutique shops and trying on the most expensive clothes. It doesn't matter whether or not you actually make a purchase.

My friend Christie did this with me because it worked so well for her in the days when she used to have to work for a living. At first it was difficult. I felt like I had a sign on my forehead blaring, "She really doesn't belong here! She can't afford a single thing here! Call the fashion police!" My inclination to look at the price tags and yell out, "What! One thousand dollars for *these* cheesy shoes?" probably didn't help much either. However, after visiting several high-end stores and making some purchases (such as a hair tie and a crystal-studded toothpick thingy), I became much more comfortable. I still can't bring myself to spend more than a couple hundred dollars on a dress, but now I can shop in places other than Target or Wal-Mart—if I choose.

- Get dressed up in a nice outfit and go mansion shopping in a posh neighborhood. Just make sure you wash your car first. On second thought, maybe you should rent a car for the day.
- On your next trip, whether you are going on vacation or just to the grocery store, rent a sporty convertible. (Don't forget your sun-glasses—even if they're the cheap kind!) This will do wonders for your mood (well, at least until you get the bill)—but really, you will prob-ably find it worth it. If you don't, then maybe you will stop feeling depressed about driving your old clunker.
- On a tight budget? Visit a trendy restaurant and split an appetizer with a friend. Or if this is not your style and you think it would just

make you feel depressed, go to the local diner and treat yourself to the grand-slam triple-whammy value meal breakfast. No matter what it consists of, it will be more filling than your customary bowl of corn flakes waiting for you at home, and it shouldn't cost more than seven or eight bucks.

- Every few months, go to a major department store and actually buy yourself an outfit you love, regardless of the price.
- Take a day off from work for no good reason other than to meet your friends for lunch and go see a movie. Declare that someday soon you will be able to do this every day if you so choose. (This worked well for me!)
- Get yourself a full-body massage every other month, and as you do, imagine you are being pampered in this way every day. (Believe me, massage therapists work their little hineys off; they deserve every dollar and a lot more!)
  If a massage is just not in your budget at the moment, stop in to a massage school and inquire about a student massage. You might be able to get one for twenty dollars or less.
- Instead of ramen noodles, buy yourself a steak and veggies or a nice cut of fish and cook your-self a full meal. Make sure you sit down at the dinner table with a candle. Give yourself a nice

bath afterward. Your body will appreciate a full, hearty meal and will reward you with the ability to manifest even more money to purchase extravagant luxuries—like food!

- Write yourself a check for a thousand, even a million, dollars, and hang it on the wall of your bedroom. I did this for my son when he was six, and within three years he had starred in three national commercials and had earned over twenty thousand dollars in residuals from less than four days of work. Not exactly a million (yet!), but we aren't complaining.
- Take out all the five-hundred-dollar bills from your Monopoly game and carry them around in your wallet as if they were real. (Just don't hand them out!)

These are just a few things you can do that will send signals to yourself that you are abundant, that you deserve to be pampered, and that you might just be on your way up in the world. Believe me: it is possible to feel like a queen from time to time, even when your wallet indicates you have less than the neighborhood bag lady.

The cool thing is after a while, your ability to manifest anything in your life will become easier, so you will be able to spend less time doing these silly exercises, although you will always have them to fall back on.

**Manifesting a creative project that sells**
Whether you wish to write and publish a book, make and sell a film, get a record deal, become a successful actor, or do and sell your art, you first need to get it out of your head that it's impossible, unlikely, far-fetched, or unrealistic to accomplish these things. The fact is, there are lots and lots of people who make a living by promoting, producing, publishing, and distributing works of art, and by representing artists. They are out there, desperately searching for people like you right now! The things you need are as follows:

1. Talent or a quality product.

2. Confidence in the quality of your work.

3. An understanding of the market your work will do well in.

4. An ability to tell people why what you are offering is unique and valuable. If you don't know, then your goal/wish should be to figure this out. The journey of discovering this will bring you further than you could imagine.

5. The initiative to put yourself in the best possible place to achieve your goal. For example, if you want to be a television or film actor, the best place for you to go is Hollywood.

If you say, "Hollywood? I'd never go there!" that's fine. But just know you may be cutting yourself off from many opportunities that will help your goal.

6. The expectation, even if everyone else thinks there's just a one-in-a-million chance for the opportunity, that *you* are the one in a million who will get this opportunity.

7. An understanding that fame and fortune may be just one new idea away, and that just by adjusting or altering the way you do things in a very minor way, you can increase your income tremendously. For example, for years I had been teaching groups of people in weekend workshops. But one day I got the idea to offer training to individuals over the telephone. Within two months I had four new students, which paid my rent for the next several months. The cool thing was I had so much fun teaching in this way that I fell in love with my work all over again. All of this came about from having a sudden idea, taking thirty minutes to make some changes on my website, and sending out one e-mail blast.

### EXERCISE

Write down a goal at the top of a piece of paper. Then write down every possible thing you can think of to do that would make it more likely your goal will be successful. Your list might include going to school or getting more training, moving to a new location, contacting certain people, or changing the way you meet or connect with clients. Don't leave anything out, small or large. Now go back and ask yourself, what on this list would I not be willing to do or am I avoiding or afraid to try or doubtful will work? Circle that thing, and look at it good and hard. That may be just the thing you *do* need to do. Then look at your list again, and circle all the things on it you can begin to do today, right now.

### EXERCISE
## Visit your creations in their future physical locations

One of my favorite things to do when I was writing my first two books was to go to bookstores, to the section where I thought my books would most likely be someday, and to visualize my books on the shelf. I would actually move around the books already there (only those that had several copies) and make space for my books. Then I'd take about five minutes and see my books there with my name on them.

Now, years later, I go back to some of these same stores, and I make a point of visiting my books on the shelf, exactly where I used to stand! Every time I pass by a bookstore, my son starts to groan and pulls me away: "Come on, Mom, why do we have to go look at your dumb books again, you have a hundred copies at home!" But I explain that by viewing the books where I had previously merely visualized them to be, it strengthens my own power of manifestation.

In the past year I've started to place my books face out on a higher shelf. Or I will put them beside books by a couple of my favorite authors and take their picture there with my cell-phone camera. When I am feeling very bold, I will move a copy of each of my books to the bestsellers section! Coincidentally (wink wink), I was recently informed that Barnes & Noble has designated my second book for a special display, meaning it's now appearing on shelves higher up, face out. Hmmm, I wonder where you'll find *this* book!

I welcome you to play around with this concept. If you are an artist, visit museums and galleries and visualize your artwork hanging on the walls. Feel how happy you are that your work is being displayed there. If you are a filmmaker, screenwriter, or actor, go to the movie theater and visualize your film appearing on the big screen. See your name in the credits and pretend you hear other people speaking excitedly about it, giving it great reviews.

***Play with time travel:*** As you stand in the place your creation is most likely to be displayed, pretend that you are yourself in the future, coming back to admire that which you created in the past. Allow you as your future self to speak words of encouragement to your past self.

Then switch over to being the past version of yourself. Send words of gratitude to your future self for sending back the encouragement to you in time. Allow yourself to receive these words and be comforted by them.

Go back and forth in time in your imagination between your past, present, and future selves, enjoying a dialog between them. Take turns being each one. This may be confusing at first but it will get easier. I really believe that these different parts do help each other out, although I can't explain the physics behind this process.

A relationship is different from a partnership: a relationship is two
people relating to each other's issues; a partnership is about two
people working together under a conscious intentional agreement
to achieve a common goal.
—Viki King

God turns you from one feeling to another and teaches you by means of
opposites, so that you will have two wings to fly—not one.
—Rumi

12

# BALANCING MASCULINE
# AND FEMININE ENERGIES

We sometimes have difficulties manifesting goals because
what can be thought of as our male (yang) and female
(yin) energies are severely out of balance. Our female
energy is that which allows us to focus inward. It's the
part of us that creates through intention, thought, and
emotion. When we meditate, pray, or repeat affirmations, we are utilizing and activating our female energy.
This is the part of us that is actively passive. We send
out an intention and then wait to receive it. We let the
intention work for us. As clairvoyants or meditation

practitioners, this is the part of ourselves that must sit in silence and wait for the information or inspiration to come in. You could also see the feminine as the spirit. Please note that receptivity is not about just sitting around doing nothing and hoping for a miracle. It has to do with establishing a clear intention based on one's intuition, and remaining alert, aware, focused, and *ready* for action.

The male energy or aspect of our self is that which is actually compelled to take physical action. It is the part that makes phone calls, sends e-mails, scans the want ads for jobs or homes or whatever it is we seek— oh yes, and takes out the garbage, if it remembers.

When these energies are well integrated and balanced within an individual, that person's life will run more smoothly, with less stress and drama. Such a person may enjoy greater harmony with romantic relationships. Through my clairvoyant readings, I have observed that many people run into problems with relationships when their own masculine or feminine energies are out of balance. This is true in both heterosexual and homosexual relationships.

### Too much masculine energy
People who overidentify with the masculine, action-oriented self tend to be too controlling and put out more effort than is needed to accomplish a task. Such people are caught in a cycle of too much doing and not

enough being. Often this obsessive "doing" is fueled by anxiety. As long as they are busy they feel they are accomplishing something. Through their busy-ness, they can avoid having to feel their feelings. This is usually at the root of most obsessive behavior and is a common trait of workaholics. Sometimes too much action is a symptom of a lack of faith. Some people believe the only way they will be able to create any kind of opportunity is through their own actions.

These people are fearful that if they don't cover every base, some opportunity might slip by. They must apply for every job in the newspaper, or visit every apartment for rent in a fifty-mile radius. Those caught in this cycle usually come to a clairvoyant out of frustration if not pure exhaustion. They know what they are doing is not working, but they don't know what else to do. They are terrified of missing an opportunity by not being in the right place at the right time. They suffer from a lack of faith.

A common image that comes to me when I am dealing with people like this is someone running on a treadmill or in circles. My usual prescription for such people is to stop all this activity and take a break. Sometimes I see they need to do some meditations, visualizations, or affirmations, but many times all it seems they need is to get lots of sleep, or even to take away their attention from the thing they want by watching TV or having fun.

You'd think people would be happy to hear that all they have to do is go home, relax, watch a movie, or go dancing, but someone with an overabundance of masculine energy won't believe this. What they don't understand is that in the course of having fun, we raise our energetic vibration, and that is what will allow goals and new opportunities, frequently wondrous ones, to flow right into our lives. Fun is a much higher vibration than stress. An hour of fun can equal if not surpass the benefits of three months of job or apartment or soul-mate searching! If this is hard for you to believe, it may be the very thing *you* need the most.

**Not enough masculine energy**

On the other hand, I've observed my share of couch potatoes, including spiritual practitioners, who have no problem sitting in a lotus position for hours, diligently saying their mantras and affirmations but barely mustering enough energy to leave the house or ask someone on a date. The prescription for these home-bodies is to get out, network, and engage in activities that are going to get their physical energy flowing. (Hello, all you silly people of the techno generation: staring into the eyes of your beloved's picture on Facebook or MySpace is not the same as staring into his or her eyes across the dinner table—although it may be less expensive!)

This message is particularly important for those of you who don't want to take any action until you are positive you know exactly what you want to do. Merely walking or driving around will sometimes give you the answer that was eluding you when you were stuck trying to figure it out in your head. Sometimes you actually do need to put your body in the right place at the right time.

### Listening to your inner female

Women throughout history have suffered because of the decisions men have made for them. Since men have traditionally been the ones who made the decisions for the entire household, a woman had to accept and then deal with the consequences of men's actions, no matter how stupid they were.

As women, it's not so much men who are oppressing us anymore as it is our very own masculine energies standing over us like the Gestapo. When the feminine within us cries out, "I don't feel like going to the office today!" or "What I really need more than anything is just to sit here and veg, daydream, or meditate," it's our masculine part that resists and warns, "You'd better shut up or you're going to get us both into trouble." A woman who listens to her intuition is in direct opposition to the masculine part of herself and to all the other men and women who have a matching set of step-by-step instructions, rule books, and laws imprinted into their brains about the most beneficial way to get ahead in life and stay there.

So when the feminine rebels and yells, "If you don't listen to me, I'm going to get sick or we're going to have an accident," the masculine will still counter, "But there isn't time, it's not practical, it's not responsible, it's not according to the schedule! But okay, fine, have it your way, just take an extra five minutes for lunch. You can make it up by coming in early tomorrow." So then what do you do? Like a good little girl or woman or man you listen to this tyrant, maybe even take a pill or a drink to shut him out or to help you forget just how tired and miserable you really are in this trap.

Sometimes when your inner female is not heard, the only thing she can do is rebel. She does this by getting sick, or by creating so much drama and noise that the person with the controlling masculine energy is forced into responding either by honoring her, abandoning her, or destroying her. This is true whether the one with the masculine energy is another person, or whether it's the most dominant part of oneself.

### Many women still want a man to do their work for them

Many women are really lacking in their masculine aspect so they seek out men who will compensate for this imbalance. (This happens with a large portion of gay men as well.)

Last month I met with three clients during the course of a twenty-four-hour period who had the same issues holding them back. One was a client of mine from the Pacific Northwest, whom I'll call Betsy. She has been separated from her husband, a successful and domineering divorce attorney, for over three years. She has been having an affair with another man, whom she referred to as her "boyfriend," for almost a decade. (You do the math.) When we began working together, she complained that her boyfriend was unwilling to spend as much time with her as she desired. It seemed he felt justified in leaving town for weeks at a time without her, with the excuse that even though she no longer lived with her husband, she was still officially married. I didn't quite buy this excuse, but I knew the only way she'd know his true intentions was to become free herself, which she needed to do anyway.

Betsy felt very "stuck" in her life on many levels. When I asked her why she didn't get divorced, she blamed her husband. She said over the past two years, every time she asked him to meet to discuss the divorce, he put it off. I asked her what her attorney thought, and she said she hadn't yet selected one, that she hadn't really been sure she needed one even though she was positive she wanted a divorce. (Okay, let me repeat: her husband is a divorce attorney, a controlling man who doesn't want to get divorced. That makes sense, let's just wait for him to draw up the deal himself!)

When we got to the bottom of things, it turned out Betsy's husband has still been fully supporting her during the past three years, with the hope she'd come back to him. While she was aware of how guilty she felt for leaving her husband, she didn't want to admit, at least to me, that money was a factor. She was waiting and relying on the very man who didn't want to let her go to set her free, and to do it in a way that would ensure she was taken care of for the rest of her life. While I can't argue that it would be nice to have income flowing in without having to work for it, I also felt that for her, needing to generate the income would be a motivating factor that would lead to positive results.

I've seen this in more than just a few friends who live off inheritances, trust-fund accounts, or alimony; these friends just don't have the same motivating factors the rest of us do to take certain steps. The need for money can be quite a powerful incentive to get off your butt and do something worthwhile! At the same time, we don't want to get dependent on the need for money to motivate us, because this sets up a vicious cycle of manifesting the need for money as opposed to eliminating that need.

In Betsy's case, she really wanted to move on with her life, but she was continuing to let her guilt, financial dependency, and the desire for someone to make things easier for her stop her in her tracks. I am not saying there sometimes isn't an easy way out, but I am noting that in many cases such women are being presented with an opportunity to be courageous, to have faith in themselves, and to accept the consequences of their actions as adults instead of as little girls.

Furthermore, by refusing to be with their husbands fully or to let the relationship go, they are keeping themselves and their husbands in an excruciating purgatory that is far more painful than it would be if they took the difficult road of going through with their divorces on their own. So many people allow their guilt to be their judge and executioner. I am not saying their husbands were perfect little angels here; but when it comes to moving forward in your life, discussions about who is right or wrong or who is the bad guy do absolutely nothing except keep you stuck. It doesn't matter who is to blame. What matters is what steps are you taking now to create the life you long for.

Please understand that I am not advocating for divorce or for leaving one's marriage. What I am saying is we really have to understand our own motivations for giving away our power. If you are truly unhappy and not willing to continue to try to make things work, it makes no sense to rely on the very person you are attempting to leave to do for you what you can't do for yourself. And of course this can be complicated by being in a relationship with someone who has encouraged you to be dependent on him or her, by convincing you to give up your own resources for the sake of the relationship or family.

## Obsession

When your feminine/masculine energies are out of balance, it's very easy to become fixated on, dependent on, or obsessed with someone who is polarized in the opposite end of the spectrum of the masculine/feminine dichotomy. If that seems to describe you or your current situation, I recommend doing the exercises below.

### EXERCISE
### Journey to meet your inner male/female

The following exercises were taught to me by one of the most awesome healers I know: Kazandrah Martin, who lives in Sedona. She healed herself of a brain tumor within a month after leaving a dysfunctional relationship.

Lie down, close your eyes, relax. Take some deep breaths. Imagine you are walking down a winding path in a peaceful forest. Visualize the foliage alongside the path. Notice how bright the sun is and how warm or cold it is; you can even visualize your feet walking.

When it feels like you have found the right spot, look around for a big stone and a flowering tree. Behind the stone you will find your inner male. Behind the tree you will find your inner female. Go to the one you feel most comfortable with first. Then sit down on the stone, or next to the tree, and relax. Wait until your inner male or female shows up. Say hello to him or her. Observe what he or she looks like. Ask this aspect how he or she feels.

Then invite this aspect to cross over to the other side of the path to meet his or her counterpart. Just sit back and watch what happens. You goal here is to observe how the two greet each other, what their appearances are like, and how they communicate.

If things don't look that great, then you can always step in. Do a little couples counseling with them. Get them to talk. Show them each a mental picture of how you'd like them to be together and individually. If your inner female or male looks weary or sickly, go ahead and hug him or her in your imagination. Promise him or her you will do everything to help with the necessary healing. Offer the assurance of your continued love. I recommend doing an energy healing on your inner female or male by following the next exercise as well. Leave them both there in the forest to begin healing their relationship, or to continue as they were if it looked really positive.

## Healing/balancing the male and female within

Close your eyes. Center yourself in a quiet place in your mind, slightly above and between your eyes. Imagine there is a third eye or window opening up in your forehead, and visualize a reading screen out about six inches from your head. A *reading screen* can look like a simple rectangle, a television screen, or a computer monitor. It gives you a place to focus your attention as you work with smaller symbols.

Once you've created a reading screen, visualize two identical, transparent roses or lotus flowers—one to the far left and one to the far right. Observe them for a moment in their starting positions. Then label one as representing your inner male, the other as your inner female. You can place the label below the flower or drop it into its own bud. Next, simply relax and observe what happens to the flowers. Notice the color, shape, and size of each one. Then ask each one to show you a personification of the energy. Just sit back and observe the flowers. Notice if either one changes. Ask them to show you the nature of their relationship. Again, just sit back and see what happens.

If you notice anything that doesn't seem optimal about their relationship, you can ask each one what he or she needs from the other. You can address them directly and invite them to respond with a verbal or auditory message and/or a visual sign. You can also invite each one to do a healing on the other. Or you can do a clairvoyant healing on both of them by visualizing a rose in the middle that represents their communication.

To do this, simply ground the communication rose by giving it a stem and seeing the stem sink deep down into the earth. Next, ask for the color of their improved communication to appear first, and then ask that any oppositional energies show themselves in the form of darker colors within the center rose. As these colors emerge, gently but firmly command them to release down the grounding cord. You can facilitate this release by pushing these colors down the cord with your imagination and will. You can also ask your inner male and female to do the healing on the communication rose. Notice how they do this and what happens.

### Results

The cool thing about all the exercises in this book is that when you release foreign energy from your body, your aura, and/or your surroundings, and then draw in your own energy or vibrations of health or peace or joy, changes occur both within yourself and in other people around you. Your feminine and masculine energies can rebalance themselves even if you aren't aware you are working directly with them. You may suddenly see things in a whole new light. Options will bloom where before they were about as hard to find as a cold can of soda in the Sahara desert. You may suddenly find the courage, strength, or incentive to speak about something or to take steps you had been avoiding. You may now find more time for meditation or work on your creative projects, or you might discover a whole new appreciation for yourself. At the same time, you will often notice that other people in your life will begin to act differently as well. There might be an initial confrontation or drastic change in the relation-ship dynamics, but usually this will quickly lead to improved relations, or perhaps the dissolution of the relationship for the betterment of both parties.

In truth everything and everyone/Is a shadow of the Beloved/
And our seeking is His seeking/And our words are His words . . .
We search for Him here and there/While looking right at Him/
Sitting by His side, we ask: "O Beloved, where is the Beloved?"
—RUMI

# 13

# HOW TO BECOME A GOD

One of the most powerful ways to awaken your inner
genie is through the act of infusing yourself with the
concept of God. You'll notice that I frame this as the
*concept of God* as opposed to just stating *God*.

I do this for a few reasons. First, the concept of
God is obviously not God in actuality, just as the
concept of an ocean is not an ocean itself or our perception of the world is not the world itself. Even the
most educated marine biologist does not know every
creature in, or understand every aspect of, the ocean;

it is too vast to know. At the time I'm writing this, everyone in my life and in the media has been talking about the state of the economy: worrying about it, thinking about it, and allowing it to influence them. But the economy is not physical—so what is it? For that matter, what is the world? And in the same vein, what is God? Since God is something so much larger than ourselves, we will never be able to come close to "figuring out" who or what God is. Fortunately, we don't need to.

In this chapter I am going to teach you how to infuse yourself with the energy of God, so you can access the infinite creative abilities ascribed to God. One day during a meditation, I asked how I could manifest a new place to live, and that is when the techniques in this chapter came to me. Not only have these techniques given me a stronger sense of power, but they have also eliminated my anxiety; within three days of that meditation, I had signed the lease for my new dream home.

Please understand, I am not trying to convert you. If I found that infusing oneself with the concept/ energy of a banana worked just as well, I'd be talking bananas here. The problem with the word *God* is that it is a symbol that has been contaminated by all the other symbols we associate with it. Just tune in to your feelings as you repeat the word to yourself: "God, God, God." What does that word elicit for you? For many it will be nice, warm, fuzzy feelings, but for others these feelings will be tinged with or overpowered by confusion, distaste, and distress. This reaction is not to the energy of God, but to our "pictures" around the word God. Some of these pictures are painful. Many people feel betrayed because God did not step in to save a loved one from death, or did not protect them from abusers during childhood. Sometimes God was forced down their throats by adults who used the name of God to control them. Many religious fanatics wouldn't recognize the energy of God if their life depended on it. That's why a lot of them end up dead before their time, as in the case of young suicide bombers.

The important thing to remember is that these memories and thoughts laden with disappointment, judgment, and pain are a completely separate thing from the energy of God. Since I don't want to program you myself, I am not even going to try to describe what my experience of the energy of God is like. Instead, I will merely describe one of the easiest ways to access this energy. Then you can decide whether or not there is something to it.

I mention all this because in order to benefit from the technique I will introduce in a little bit, it's necessary first to let go of your preconceptions, confusion, or repulsion to the idea of God.

## Overcoming resistance to the God symbol

I think a clue to understanding the power of the God symbol lies in one of the definitions of the word *law*. A law is a rule that describes but does not explain a pattern in nature, and predicts what will happen under specific conditions. So if we think of God as a law, let's call that law "the law of God"—and then we might define this law as, "When a person infuses themselves with the concept, energy, idea, or symbol of God, that person's life will restructure itself to form a pattern of greater harmony." Notice here the law isn't at all attempting to explain how or why this all works, only that when one activity is carried out it will have a certain effect.

The nice thing about this is we can stop trying to figure out something that our puny brains will never be able to understand, and instead get right down to taking care of business—the business of drawing our wishes to us and seeing our needs fulfilled, so that our lives become far more pleasurable and easier to navigate.

## Trying to understand keeps us stuck!

Our minds are like moths, constantly fluttering around trying to find the light even when the light is coming from a source that will burn them the moment they land. As babies we are taught words paired together as contradictions. Two of the first words an English-speaking child learns are *yes* and *no*. Then come *good* and *bad*, and *boy* and *girl*. Yet this is a function and perception of our minds, not of things as they really are. We as humans are programmed early on to categorize, label, and judge. It is through these lenses that we view our world, our lives, each other, and ourselves.

Our minds are like an insane filing clerk who must find the correct file immediately and then check and recheck to make sure the information is placed in the correct folder. Luckily, the filing cabinet is not really that big, since everything could potentially fall into the categories of *bad* or *good*, at least within our own system. Things begin to get shaken up when we compare our filing systems to those of others in our lives, and discover that for them, the same information (e.g., ideas and opinions about communism, a particular song or movie, your husband) has been placed in the opposite folders.

Then we become like two frightened and confused filing clerks with obsessive-compulsive disorder, battling it out on top of the Xerox machine that keeps spitting out the same blank piece of paper.

When it comes to the idea of God, our inner filing clerks insist they know exactly which file this idea goes in and will slap or kill you if you try to tell them otherwise; or else they are confused, jumping from folder to folder and unable to find the right one.

Have you ever wondered what would happen if you lit a match to all those files and fired the clerk?

I think I know. You'd experience silence, peace, nothingness. At least for a few moments, until the unfamiliar silence startled you and you ran back to find the clerk in hopes of a possible reconciliation. After all, it took you a long time to accumulate these files. Some of them are even entertaining. What's there to do without them?

When we meditate or play a musical instrument, we are sometimes able to step out of the filing room and achieve short periods of this silence. Another way—easier for some, harder for others—is simply to become aware of our inner clerks and files and move away from them. This means we become aware that all these attempts to categorize, judge, figure out, blame, accuse, dissect, theorize, assume, label, solve, and analyze are tricks of the mind and may be futile. They may not be bringing us even one step closer to really understanding or knowing anything—whether that "anything" is God, the truth, our spouse, or the best course of action to take. Instead, our insistence on duality may be keeping us from experiencing life fully. The next time you find yourself judging or comparing two things, ask yourself what you are hoping or needing to find. Why must anything be considered better than something else? The only reason we need to make others wrong is so we can feel "right" or justify our own actions. There is absolutely no other reason.

Can we be right without ever making a comparison or judgment? Yes and no. The idea of being right is itself a fallacy. It does not exist; rather, it's a symptom and need manufactured by the ego. The more judgmental and analytical people are, the more insecure and judgmental they are of themselves, and the weaker they and their ability to manifest becomes. However, what we *can* do is be who we are. Whether that is right or wrong in someone else's mind or our own mind is not the question and is insignificant. In this respect, Descartes couldn't have been further off base when he said, "I think, therefore I am."

What I'd like you to do right now is let go of the need to have God explained, and instead allow yourself to fully experience the power of God as a "pattern in nature," one that permits us to predict what will happen under specific conditions. The conditions will be as follows:

### EXERCISE
### God as a magic symbol

1. Create a grounding cord: Visualize your first chakra, which you can see as a spinning disk corresponding to the cervix or inner pelvic region. Visualize a column of blazing energy

running from this energy center all the way down to the center of the earth.

2. Next, ask yourself this question: "What do I picture when I think of God?" Warning! Don't try to judge and alter this perception before it comes in. What we are really looking for here is your unconscious picture of God. So ask yourself: when I usually think of God, what does she or he look like? Do you see an old man with a beard? A scrawny man who resembles George Burns, smoking a cigar? Perhaps a goofy guy making funny faces who reminds you of Jim Carrey in the film *Bruce Almighty*? Or do you see a cross or a star or a column of light? Do you see God above you? Do you see a light in your heart?

    Now, out in front of you, form a screen like a television set, movie screen, computer monitor, or a blank sheet of paper (if you've read my other books, I refer to this as a *reading screen*). On the screen, let your most common image of God appear.

3. Next, postulate that you yourself are God. So go ahead and now replace your vision of God that you just conjured up in step 2 with a vision of yourself. See yourself as if you were looking at yourself in a mirror.

4. Continue seeing yourself as God by putting your attention back on your body. Center yourself within your heart. Say "Hello, God" to your own heart, and continue to hold a picture of yourself as you are right now.

5. Begin contemplating the abilities that God or you as God might have. These could include power, the ability to create anything immediately, omniscience, omnipresence, and an endless capacity for love, peace, joy, and so on. So if you previously visualized God as a ball of light or an old bearded man, now replace these images with your own smiling face.

6. Imagine that you are opening up a photo album. On the first page is a blank picture. Under it there is a label that reads God. Place an image of your face as the single image in the photo. Then write your name over the word God so that the names coexist in the same place. Meditate on this picture for as long as possible. Then turn the page. You will notice that every page has your picture with a label containing your name and God's name simultaneously.

7. The key here is to meditate on the image of yourself as God—not like God, or a part of God, but as God! Then begin saying to yourself, in your mind, the mantra, "I am God, I am God,

we are the same." After you do this a hundred times or close to it, begin repeating this mantra out loud. Start off saying it quietly, then let the volume increase, until you are yelling it as loudly as possible. If you are fearful someone might hear you, then go find an isolated spot where you can yell this out as loudly as possible for at least a minute. You can bring the volume down until it's barely audible, then move it back into your head. While you do this, keep seeing yourself as God.

8. Here comes the activation part. Visualize yourself as God emanating the light of God. The light of God will beam through you. The light is the bigger part of the God-self that created you in the first place and that gives you your energy and the God power. It's like you are the God lamp and this is the battery. You can also think of this light as a breath moving through God's body. This breath is God's breath and your own breath. So as your breath, you are breathing God's light through your God body. This has a powerful impact and also helps cover all the bases, so your mind doesn't go into confusion about being God when it might not feel as powerful as it should. It's the light beaming through you and breathing through you as God that fully activates your God powers.

9. Begin, or continue if you've already started, to visualize the brightest, most blinding light you can envision emanating from the core of you within your body. See it streaming outward in all directions, beaming out like light through stained glass from your center, through all parts of your body, past your body, and as far out as you can imagine it. Just when you can't imagine it getting any brighter, amp it up another few notches in your imagination. You can use the visualization that your body is the glass and the God-light beams through you as the glass, shining out far, in all directions, gloriously and triumphantly for all the world and people of the world to see. (Perhaps this is why so many churches have such large stained-glass windows.) Be God, breathing God's breath and beaming God's light through every cell and every pore of your body. This is the activation. You can see this happening directly to your body and you can view this all on your screen. Let your attention go back and forth from you, centered in your body, to the mirror image of your body on the screen.

10. The final step is to remind yourself that you and God are a pair, a combination that will set you and your inner genie free. This symbol is

a key, a code, like that on your garage, front gate, or even your voicemail. Once you punch in the password, these devices open with no effort. Postulate that God as a universal symbol, energized by the masses who worship this symbol, will unlock the powers of creation, creativity, and manifestation within you. You may find that if you do this exercise before any of the others in this book, your results may be even more magnified. You are now completely primed for success.

## Homework assignment

For at least one week, do this exercise at least once a day, preferably in the morning. It would be great to conjure it up as you go about your day, all week long. Notice what happens to your day and your life. I guarantee you will see results. But look out—initially, you may begin to release a lot of negative emotions, so don't be surprised if you go through a period of emotional intensity. This will give way to that which you seek.

*You have enemies? Good.*
*That means you've stood up for something, sometime in your life.*
*—WINSTON CHURCHILL*

# 14

# REMOVING OTHER PEOPLE'S INFLUENCE FROM OUR CREATIONS

### Energetic influences from individuals

If our own thoughts and feelings are energies that can attract our desires to us, then others' thoughts and feelings are also powerful magnets that can and do impact us as well. I am certain that the way we feel about ourselves, the risks we are willing or not willing to take, many of the decisions we make or don't make, and many of the actions we take or don't take are impacted by others' thoughts and feelings, whether or not we are aware of it. Many times others' opinions of us or their fears for us are lodged within our auric fields. These impact us physically, emotionally, cognitively, and spiritually.

People can transmit negative thoughts and emotions from thousands of miles away, and we often pick up on these thoughts and emotions, mistaking them for our own. In this way, we are all being naturally psychic all the time. As I am sure you know, most of the time it's not that these people are trying to keep us from moving forward or achieving our goals; sometimes, most of the time, it's out of their love and concern for us that they project their fears onto us. Their fears then become our own or exacerbate our own. This keeps us trapped in a cycle of apathy, confusion, or exhaustion. Then there are, of course, people who flow in (and hopefully out of) our lives who do have opposing agendas and very much want to stop us from reaching our goals.

*Whether these projected fears are coming from someone who loves us or someone who hates us makes little difference.* Both kinds of projections can interfere with the law of attraction and our ability to manifest. The closer we are to people (typically such people include parents, siblings close to our age, or someone we've had sexual intercourse with) on an emotional and physical level, the more we are impacted by their thoughts, both positive and negative. Also, the more people we have projecting emotionally charged thoughts toward us, the stronger the impact. This of course can work two ways. When people are sending us thoughts of love, light, and healing, we may receive a powerful healing and overcome all sorts of ailments. When they are sending angry, hurtful thoughts, it can really wear us down. One of the main reasons people suffer from confusion is because they have too much of other people's energy circulating through their heads. It's hard to hear your inner voice when there are so many people yelling at you from within.

## How to tell if you are
### being impacted by others' energies

So how do we know if we are being blocked by resistance in the form of other energies, or if we are being blocked by ourselves, perhaps by something hidden deep in our subconscious? I've seen far too many psychics and healers caught up in the blame game of feeling like they are being psychically attacked or thwarted, when in actuality the culprit was really their own emotional pain, fear, or low self-esteem. I've also seen many psychology students or professionals who were so fixated on unraveling the mysteries of their own unconscious processes that they wasted a lot of time trying to fix themselves when there was nothing to fix, but rather something that needed to be released. It's kind of like walking around with an axe in your head and wondering why your years of therapy or medication aren't taking away the pain!

One of the most helpful things a clairvoyant reader can do is look to see what exactly is getting in the way of one's ability to manifest or successfully apply the law of attraction, and essentially discover if there is an axe in a client's head. If there is, the clairvoyant discovers how best to remove it, how it got there in the first place, how it might be impairing the person, and perhaps traces it back to who put it there and why they were able to get it past the client's natural defenses. However, visiting a clairvoyant is not essential either for the diagnosis of any of our problems or for the treatment. There are some signs you can be aware of that frequently indicate there is a foreign energy that is inhibiting the magnetism of your mind:

1. First, ask yourself if you are aware of anyone or anything in particular that is blatantly standing in the way of you and your wishes and goals. What do you find? Perhaps a parent, spouse, or boss telling you they will not let you do what you'd like to do, why it won't work, or how you might get hurt or hurt them? Next, ask yourself if, when you have any discouraging thoughts about going ahead with your dreams, you tend to hear the doubts as if they were spoken in the voice of someone you know, or if you find yourself having conversations with a particular person in your head explaining, defending, or

making your case. Ask yourself, who is the first person that comes to mind whenever you think about doing something you've been longing to do? Does thinking about this person motivate you to pursue your dreams or to shove them under the rug?

2. Another sign that you may be picking up on others' energy occurs when you are initially very excited about what you are creating, about the steps you are taking to move toward your goals, but suddenly all the air is let out of your balloon. You feel discouraged, and you may even cancel your plans or turn down the opportunities you've been waiting for. You have no idea what has brought on this sudden change of heart. Of course you might just be encountering your own fears, so this needs to be considered in correlation with the rest of the signs.

3. Just as you are about to take a step or get what you want, people suddenly pop up with problems they expect you to deal with. The more it seems like you are their only hope, the more you can be sure this is a sign of energetic resistance standing in between you and your ability to manifest.

4. You plan to spend time doing manifesting meditations, but then something happens. You fall

asleep, get distracted, or get an offer to do something more pressing—like scrub the kitchen
floor or watch a rerun of *Jeopardy*. Notice who
shows up to give you something else to do.

5. You find yourself experiencing an extreme
   emotion that overtakes you, and that you can't
   shake no matter what you do. You find yourself
   behaving in ways you normally wouldn't; for
   example, you find yourself throwing objects
   or becoming violent, but only when you are
   around one particular person.

### Why would others, consciously or unconsciously, not want us to manifest?

- They are afraid we will leave them.
- Competition. They don't want us to have what
  they don't think they can have. They are envious. They are satisfied by feeling superior.
- Limits. Many of our loved ones are thoroughly
  convinced only certain things are possible. If
  we exceed the limits they set for themselves
  and ourselves, then this undermines their
  entire version of reality, and makes it more
  difficult for them to maintain their excuses as
  to why they are not taking steps to empower
  themselves in their own lives. Anytime we
  begin to exceed the limits of those who raised

us or even the society we come from, we are prone to hit resistance.

- Agendas. Other people may not want us to manifest because they have a plan for us they want us to follow. They want to be in control.

### The spirit world

You may not believe in them, but I have no doubt whatsoever that we are constantly receiving information from spirits and nonphysical entities. These beings can have a profound impact on our thoughts, emotions, and self-esteem, thereby influencing our creations. It's not a matter of whether they are positive or negative, as much as it is that many of them have their own agendas, while some just can't help being a pain in the ass, as that's their nature. In this respect, they are not really any different from spirits with bodies—i.e., people.

There are some abusive spirits out there that spew curses and other disparaging words, emotions, and energetic frequencies at people. Some people can actually hear this communication as voices that they recognize as coming from a source outside themselves, while others hear it as their own voice. Those belonging to the first group might fear they are going insane, which might be what the troublesome entity is striving for. Those who hear it as their own voice will likely suffer from depression and low self-esteem. Both groups of people may be vulnerable to suicidal ideation. I am convinced that some spirits actually try to lead people down the road of killing themselves or others. Thankfully, there are spirits on the opposite end of this spectrum giving us encouragement and seeking to protect us from these invisible bullies.

From the plethora of experiences I've had as a clairvoyant, I've found that spirits can be found along a spectrum of light and darkness. Light by its very nature moves in an outward direction. It spreads and illuminates whatever is near. Darkness absorbs. The darker something is, the more it sucks in the light. Notice I am not calling one or the other "bad" or "good"; I am merely describing their qualities as I experience them. Spirits that are all light therefore have an energizing effect. Spirits that are mostly or all dark have a draining effect. This is true whether the spirit has a body, as a living human being does, or whether it dwells only in spirit form. Spirits with less light attach themselves to living humans of a similar caliber, and then together they act like a black hole, creating chaos, drama, and pain in order to receive attention from others.

What we give attention to, we give our energy to, so the more someone demands our attention, the more that person is feeding off of our energy fields. Parents who fit this description often do this to their children from the time they are born. This establishes a vicious cycle in the child's life, setting the child up as a caretaker and one who will be vulnerable to enslavement by other dark beings later in life. Often children of these types of parents are sickly, and blame themselves for problems at home.

I know this isn't the most pleasant topic to discuss, but I feel it's essential to do so. When we don't have enough of our energy, not only are we vulnerable to illness but we also have an extremely hard time manifesting. Awareness gives us the power to recognize the energy dynamics that may be keeping us stuck and to extract these people from our lives, or us from theirs. The good news is that most entities on the darker end of the continuum need a human host to work through, which means they are not just going to start bugging you for no apparent reason. Occasionally they will attach themselves to a certain location, as in house hauntings, but even then it seems as though most poltergeist activity centers around a particular person who is either having emotional problems, running strong sexual energies that may be misguided, abusing drugs and/or alcohol, or has a fascination with these types of beings.

For more information on protecting yourself from troublesome entities, you can read my second book, *Extraordinary Psychic: Proven Techniques to Master Your Natural Psychic Abilities*. There is also a classic book by Dion Fortune called *Psychic Self-Defense* that I highly recommend. The following exercises will assist in helping you to protect and clear your creations from interference from disembodied spirits and humans alike.

## Maximize attraction/minimize resistance using your clairvoyance

1. Close your eyes. Take some deep, slow breaths. Bring your attention to the center of your head. Imagine you are looking out your third eye. Visualize a gigantic, clear, transparent rose. Tell this rose it is going to represent the thing you'd like to create for yourself. You can imagine that you are writing the name of this thing beneath the rose. Ask the rose to show you the color of that which you are going to create. You can also drop some symbols inside the rose that represent it (for example, a relationship, money, a car, a trip, and so on) and watch to see what happens next. Give the rose a stem, and see the stem automatically burrow downward into the earth to secure itself.

2. Next, ask for any colors to appear that represent energy that is not in agreement for you to have this creation. Once you see the colors, visualize them releasing down the stem into the earth. Notice if the main color of your rose changes as you do this. Focus all your attention on the rose. If your mind wanders, just bring it

back to the rose as soon as you notice you've drifted off. You might have to redirect your attention a couple of times before completing this exercise. The more foreign energies involved, the more distracted you will be.

3. Bring your attention back to the color that represents what you are creating. The important thing here is you don't want to focus too much on the energy coming out; instead, focus on the color that represents what you are creating. See the color circulating, growing brighter, bolder, more sparkly and vibrant as it pushes out the oppositional energy. You can watch this rose grow bigger and bigger, and then you can see yourself in this rose, receiving what you want and feeling so happy that you are receiving it. It's very important to feel the emotions of happiness, gratitude, and excitement in conjunction with visualizations and affirmations.

4. Once you are satisfied that you have created the rose and released the resistance, you can cut the stem and let the rose float off into the universe to do its work. You can also imagine that the hands of God or your creator or another deity of your choice are above you. As you cut the rose, imagine that your wondrous creation is landing right into your deity's hands.

One of my personal favorite deities is the Hindu goddess Lakshmi. She is the goddess of prosperity and beauty. She appears as a beautiful Indian deity with several hands that hold jewels or gold bars, and she is often surrounded by peacocks. You can visualize her and ask her to bless your creation. She spontaneously appears to me from time to time. Another Hindu deity that has appeared to me, even before I knew who he was, is Ganesh. Ganesh looks like a man with a big elephant head. He represents the eliminator of obstacles. If you encounter a lot of resistance or are not convinced that the opposing energy is releasing down the grounding cord of your rose, you can ask Ganesh to step in and give the rose, and you, a healing. Jesus and Mother Mary are energies that are always there to help you. Just visualize them out in front of you, imagine you are showing them your rose with your creation, and ask them to bless it for you. Then observe what happens next.

Lakshmi and Ganesh appeared to me before I had the foggiest idea who they were. As I discuss in my book *You Are Psychic*, Jesus and Mary have spontaneously appeared during the course of my work with clients. On some of these occasions, other psychics who were present or in different parts of the building observed these figures at the exact same time I was experiencing them.

## Discover how certain people impact your creations

Once you are in a quiet place in your mind, centered behind your third eye, imagine you are looking out of your third eye onto a screen that resembles a computer monitor, blackboard, whiteboard, movie screen, or piece of white paper. On one side of the screen, visualize a clear, transparent rose. Ask it to fill up with the energy of the thing you are hoping to attract. Look at the color, shape, and size of the rose, and any other qualities about the leaves or the stem that may show themselves.

Next to this, on the other side of your screen, put up an image of your mother, father, or spouse. You can see them as figures of people or visualize another transparent rose and invite that person's energy to come into it and show itself as a color. Next, move the person or the receptacle filled with the person's energy close up to the rose representing your creation, and watch what happens when that person comes into contact with your creation. You might even introduce them to your manifestation by saying, "Dad, I'd like you to meet the boyfriend I am creating," or "Mom, I'd like you to meet the thousands of dollars I am manifesting," or "Honey, what do you think of this new job that will be in my life any day now?" Then, just sit back and watch what happens with your rose. First, look to see if it changes colors in any way. The color is the beginning step that will give you something to focus your attention on. Once you notice a change in the rose, you can ask it to give you more detailed information through additional images or even messages.

You may notice quite a bit of change to your rose, or you may notice nothing at all. If you are not pleased with what you see, move on to the next exercise, and understand that this may be telling you it's better not to discuss your manifestation with the person in question until you've actually attracted your manifestation fully into your life.

Sometimes we think someone is supportive of what we are trying to do. That person may in fact be supportive, but his or her unconscious doubts or fears could still be influencing us. It's important not to judge someone who seems to be inadvertently influencing you or to view this behavior as an attack, because such a judgment will only slow you down even more. At some point in your life, your energy has impacted others around you in the same way.

Remember the expression *What you resist, persists?* Try to be as neutral or as understanding as possible about another's influence *and* at the same time do what you need to do to clear that influence. This may involve working further with the energy, or it may require some action. When you live or work with someone on a daily basis, you are both living within each other's fields, and sometimes it isn't possible to clear energy from yourself or your creations until you have physically separated yourself from the other person's sphere of influence. I will discuss this more in the next chapter.

Here's the good news: If you noticed your rose being influenced in any way, that means you were using your clairvoyant ability to access this information. Congratulations! You just performed a clairvoyant reading without even realizing it.

## Shielding your manifestation

If it looks like your manifestation is vulnerable to other people's energies that are close to you or were at one time, or you suspect your manifestation might be vulnerable, then you can put up a shield that is programmed either to protect your manifestation from a specific person or from any number of people. Here's how to do it:

Visualize a clear, transparent rose and invite the energy of the thing you are wishing to manifest into that rose. Sit back, relax, and ask for a color to show itself that represents the rose. If you don't see a color, you can just assign it one. Next, choose a symbol for the thing you desire and visualize this symbol in your rose as well. In your imagination, see a stem running from the rose into the ground.

Next to this, at least a few inches away, place a symbol of the person, people, or spirit that you feel might interfere with your creation. Imagine that you are securing a mirror to the outside of the rose that represents your manifestation. See this mirror facing the people who might be impacting your creations, so that any of their interfering energy will immediately bounce back to them. You can also choose a color for their energy, and watch it float back to them or down your grounding cord just in case their energy has already entered your manifestation.

Another thing you can do is imagine you are holding a spray bottle of a substance called "exterminator protection fluid." Note that this substance will automatically repel the attention or energy of anyone who comes near your creation on an energy level. Imagine that you are lavishly spraying this fluid on your rose containing that which you wish to manifest, much as an exterminator would do to eradicate and prevent the infestation of any little critters in your backyard or house. See a color coming out of the spray bottle and watch the color completely saturate your receptacle and form a protective layer. You can also imagine you are looking at an expiration date on this bottle, which will establish for your subconscious how long this will work. The expiration date could be any number of years from now.

Only time can heal your broken heart,
just as only time can heal his broken arms and legs.
—Miss Piggy

# 15

# MANIFESTING FOR OTHERS

**Manifesting as a couple vs. as a single person**
I have learned the hard way that we can co-create *with* others but not *for* them. Also, I've learned that most conflicts that arise within relationships have to do with one's level of "havingness." Anyone who has transitioned from being a single person to one with a live-in partner will know what I'm talking about. Not only do you have the obvious challenges of dealing with different habits, preferences, needs, and desires, but you may be dealing with someone whose style

of manifesting is completely different from yours. Of course, you may have attracted a partner who was also well-versed in the laws of attraction, perhaps even more so than you. In hooking up with this partner, creating will most likely be even easier than before. If that's the boat you are in, congratulations! The power the two of you have together is tremendous. There is very little you cannot co-create together.

However, if your partner only knows how to create from effort, stress, compulsive action, or stubborn attachment to a specific outcome, you are going to have your hands full. (Believe me, you are not alone!) In this case, you will need to be extra strong. If your partner has less faith, is less open to receiving, and has much lower expectations and personal limits than you do, then you have some extra challenges ahead. If this is the case, and you love your partner enough for other reasons to want to remain with him or her, then you are going to need to decide what it is *you* want to create, whether for yourself or for you both as a couple. Then you are going to have to go at it on your own until what you desire has manifested for you, which it will, as long as you don't allow yourself to get distracted.

All this is not to say your partner won't be helpful or back you up or enjoy what you create once the bulk of the preparation work is done. *The key here is to make sure you don't lower your expectations of what you can have for yourself, and that you don't wait for your partner to do for you what you really need to do yourself.* If you are feeling frustrated or inhibited as a couple, ask yourself whether you are waiting for your partner to do the inner and outer work you could be doing right now on your own.

As challenging as it may be, it is quite possible for you to live with someone and manifest your desires even when these desires are in seeming conflict with, or in opposition to, your partner's. What I suggest is to focus solely on the things you wish to manifest and then see your partner at home looking very happy and content. Visualize your partner in the state you'd ultimately like him or her to be in.

### Finding a place to live

If you believe that you can, should, and will live in a really nice home, while your partner is thinking about a studio apartment with wallpaper made up of pages from *Sports Illustrated*, I suggest you do the exercises for manifesting in this book on your own, and then take whatever action you need to further bring yourself to your goals. In the case of house or apartment hunting, you may actually need and want to be the one to do the bulk of the footwork. Find the perfect scenario for yourself and then once it's all set up and ready to go, spring it on your partner. The worst thing you can do is insist your partner go from place to place with you, because it will only stress out your partner, and he or she will whine, complain, and try to convince you that you are out of your mind with your highfalutin ideals.

This is where many people, particularly women, go wrong. As you have already no doubt noticed, many men, at least straight men, don't like to shop unless they have a lot of extra cash in their pockets, or unless shopping involves something they will soon put in their stomach, tool box, or computer. This is true of bigger purchases like homes as well, particularly when the man involved has doubts as to whether he will be successful in obtaining the home. However, we women have this romantic notion that the man in our life should be by our sides through the whole process of manifesting our desires, in this case a home—from envisioning it to talking about it to shopping for it to moving in and decorating it. We want our men to be involved, or at least interested and supportive, in just about everything that is important to us. Not only that, but we really want our guys to do the things that we don't want to do or are uncomfortable doing on our own, particularly when we are feeling stressed or overwhelmed. If you make the mistake of insisting a partner come along with you who has a lower ability to manifest for himself than you do, then he will either sabotage your efforts out of his own fear or he may be inclined to accept the first thing that comes along that seems adequate. (By the way, I'm using male pronouns here to simplify things; please mentally replace these with female pronouns if your partner is a woman.)

*As a conscious manifester, settling for "adequate" when it comes to a place to live or a job that will take up your precious time and energy should never be an option!* What you are seeking is the extraordinary—the thing that makes you gasp in wonder and appreciation and self-congratulation every time you see or think about it! Once you find this thing, your significant other, if he is not a total creep, will be happy for you. If he isn't, because he thinks it's going to cost too much and he doesn't have the faith that you do that you can manifest the cash to pay for it, then once again it is going to be on your shoulders to come up with a way to prove him wrong.

It's not fair or wise to push our partner past his limits or too far out of his comfort zone when we are refusing to do the same. This is true especially when it comes to spending our partner's hard-earned money. If we are going to insist on having the very best, we need to be able to be the ones to financially support having the best, whether that means we are paying for the extra slack ourselves, or manifesting the resources and opportunities to make this thing work. This is how we change our partner's mind, by setting an example. So if you are in a situation where your partner is the one paying all the bills, with all the cash, but has a much lower level of what he can allow himself to have, then you are in for a challenge. Such a situation may require you to manifest your own cash flow.

## Don't go overboard!

People occasionally get so caught up in the idea that they can manifest anything that they get themselves into situations for which they are not yet ready. While I believe you can create as you go along, if you currently have no income or only a minimum-wage job, you will be putting yourself into a very stressful situation if you find a place to live that costs four thousand dollars per month! I know more than a few single people and couples who have fallen into this trap. As I've discussed in other chapters, you may not yet really have the self-esteem, the understanding, or a high enough vibration to consistently create the amount of money you'd need for that kind of mortgage. A lot of people love the idea of the law of attraction, but have not yet done the inner work necessary to make it work. That is why I've written this book!

Another problem people encounter is that they don't do enough investigation to see what they are getting themselves into. They don't do the math or read the fine print, and they end up agreeing to pay far more than they are comfortable with as a result. Remember what I said in chapter 2? There is a huge difference between having faith and having blind faith. Bad decisions come from blind faith and ignoring what is. My suggestion is to start on a smaller scale. It's one thing if you do have a cash flow, but if you are completely broke and you live in a crummy apartment, you can work on manifesting a nice home that costs the same, even less, or just slightly more, rather than setting your sights on a million-dollar mansion with a huge mortgage. I am not saying you should rule out the mansion completely; rather, if you are going to set your sights on manifesting it, then perhaps include the intention that it will come rent-free or mortgage-free—and see what shows up.

I've known several couples who ended up living for free on the most beautiful estates as caretakers, house sitters, or pet sitters, or just because the owner liked them a lot. Sometimes our more cautious and thrifty partner may be more on target than we are. We are often attracted to people who balance us out. There is a fine line between optimism and foolish, outright delusion—particularly when you are gambling with your money or putting it into risky investments you know nothing about!

**Stepping off our path and onto someone else's**
Sometimes we wake up to find that we have stepped off our own path, and onto someone else's. This is an image I've gotten several times when doing a relationship reading for a client or friend who was having a very difficult time. This happens quite frequently when we first fall in love or begin to cohabitate with a person. We are so "into" the other person that we merge into this person!

The more unhappy we were with our life before we met our partner, the easier it will be to relinquish our own path for our partner's path. In this scenario, you may give up your own place, activities, friends, and interests in exchange for his, and at first this will seem great. But then sometime down the road you may find that your own prosperity stops and you are more and more reliant on your partner, and you have somehow lost control of your own life. In dreams this is usually depicted by riding in a car that is out of control, with someone else in the driver's seat who is driving in a way that is not comfortable to you as you sit in the back seat. Of course, this situation is more likely to arise if your partner is naturally demanding or controlling.

The good news is that reclaiming your life can be fairly easy. The key here is to remove your attention from your partner's conflicts, issues, and dramas, and put every ounce of your energy into your own personal goals. That may seem quite overwhelming at first. It might require you to do some visualizations that help you call your energy out of your partner's field and back to your own, or to cut some of the cords between you. Making sure you get plenty of alone time will help you get reacquainted with yourself and what you really want within the relationship and outside of it. The important thing here is also to make sure you can go about doing what you need to do for yourself, while *allowing* your partner to have his feelings about what you are doing.

## Stop seeking constant approval
## and permission from your partner!

One of the most important lessons I and millions of other women (and some men) are learning is that it's really, truly okay if our partner doesn't approve of everything we do, say, like, or want. *The need for that approval is what enslaves us and keeps us stuck.* I know it's not easy to have your significant other moping around the house, grumbling because he is feeling neglected, threatened, or less powerful because you are taking steps toward something that is really important to you and your own emotional, spiritual, and mental health. But your partner's feelings, in the short term, should not and cannot be your problem when those feelings are a reflection of personal insecurities—providing you have done all you can do to let your partner know he is loved.

We often seek out the approval of our partner because we are not feeling confident or motivated enough to make a decision or take action on our own.

## Never put your own spiritual growth
## on hold for the sake of your relationship

People who are cut off from their spirit and spiritual abilities are initially going to have a hard time understanding why it's important for their significant other to spend money and time on "frivolous" things such as attending a spiritual-development class, reading books on spiritual growth, or even meditating. So, if you are married to or partnered with that kind of person, what do you do? Arguing or explaining won't do anything but frustrate you, because you and your mate will be speaking two different languages. Do you just throw in the towel and spend the rest of your life wishing your partner would change? I've got a better idea . . .

You must do what you need to do for yourself, trusting that over time your partner will notice the positive impact these things have on you and on your relationship together. For example, let's say (theoretically, of course) that every once in a while you begin acting like a crazed hyena. During one of these rare hysterical moments, let's say that instead of biting your partner's head off, you excuse yourself, go into your room, close your eyes, sit still, and then come back as the sweet and wonderful person you truly are. After this happens a few times your partner is not only going to notice the benefits of meditation, but he will beg you to do more of it. Likewise, when he sees that your income has quadrupled and that you have no problems in your life except for him and all his problems, he will start to wonder if maybe there isn't something about this law of attraction thing after all.

In other words, we must give our significant other a chance to give us a chance.

## Energy vampires

There are, of course, some people who are so insecure or controlling they can't bear the thought that you would go someplace without them. When you meditate (which is what you're doing when you take the time to go inward and visualize your goals), you do temporarily shut out everyone from your attention. *Nothing is wrong with that!* In fact, the more you connect with yourself, the better you will be in all your relationships. Do you feel guilty when you close the door to go to the bathroom by yourself? Do you feel guilty when you go to sleep at night, and the world, along with your partner, disappears? No, of course not. Then why should you feel bad about taking a break from the ones you love from time to time?

When you put your focus on your own spirit, that which is not you begins to drop off. When you took your marriage vows (assuming you're married), you agreed to love your spouse in sickness and in health. But did you agree to let your spouse suck out every drop of your blood until you were sick and in poor health? Did you agree to sell your very soul so as not to offend your spouse, or make your spouse have to rethink his or her own views about life? No, I think not! Parasitic people aren't going to like it one bit when you move away from them, because they will sense you are about to kick them out of your space and therefore they may not be able to suffocate you with their own will. If you are attached to this sort of person, you will have to work twice as hard to be disciplined when it comes to bringing yourself to do the work that will ultimately help you get yourself back.

### Running your own energy

See yourself surrounded in a big ball of blazing light. See yourself and your cells as if they each have an opening, a little spot that is hungry for new life. Then begin to call back your energy. See this energy as one unifying color. Start to visualize this color moving out of all the places it was healing, solving, controlling, and trying to figure out. See it moving back to you, and filling up all the empty spaces in your cells. Once your cells fill up all the way, let your energy fill up every part of your body. Now see it moving from your feet to your head, and vice versa. Allow it to go wherever it feels good: just make sure you see it moving within and around you.

### Manifesting within the organizations you work with

From the moment you accept a position with anyone or any business, you are agreeing to participate in an energy exchange. When you accept a position, whether or not you sign an official contract, you are implementing a verbal contract that includes not only your job responsibilities but also to what extent you are agreeing to give up your freedom in exchange for a paycheck. When you agree that you will show up at the same time every day to work and that you will take your breaks at a certain time for a certain number of minutes, you are essentially agreeing to put your employer's desires over the needs of your own body. You are plucking off part of your crown and replacing it with theirs. Quite often, you are agreeing to turn down the volume on the speakers to your inner voice and agreeing to allow someone else's inner genie to rule over your own. Most of the time, you relinquish these things knowingly, somewhat placated by the idea that you will have a small cushion of sick time and vacation days in addition to a paycheck, to lesson the harshness of your servitude.

Not only do you sign away your rights to your time, but you often give up your rights to be your individual self. The only way to be safe, successful, or even last for a week in this new environment is by finding a way to fit in. So we don a mask and a suit that make us indistinguishable from everyone else in the office, and we put aside those parts of ourselves that might possibly stand out and draw too much attention or criticism. Sometimes this means hiding our sense of humor or hiding our spiritual beliefs and practices; sometimes it means hiding our sexual orientation. It almost always means hiding our successes and projects outside of work (if we even have enough energy left over by the end of the week to engage in them), because these will threaten our bosses more than anything else.

Our bosses want us to be faithful to them. When they hire us, they do so because they want to make sure we will not stray. They want to make sure we will work hard for them but not show them up. If there is the slightest chance we have more experience than they do, we will immediately be disqualified from the position and branded as "overqualified." This is another way of describing a person who cannot be trusted, because such a person knows enough not to be willing to accept the control and bullshit that a less experienced or confident person would allow.

Many people even agree to give up their decency and ethics when they go to work for someone else. They do whatever their boss tells them to do, even if this means oppressing others, harassing them, or ignoring their pleas for help. Such "others" could be customers, members of the public, or fellow co-workers. Not only do these employees do the dirty work of their employers (whether private corporations or government agencies), but they also agree to soak up all the anger, resentment, and fear that come their way as a result of the company's unbending policies. This is not at all by chance but rather carefully designed to protect those at the top.

Why do we agree to participate in such a sinister process? Some of us believe it is fair because, well, at least they are giving us the chance to earn some money, right? Having a job is a privilege, isn't it? Anyway, what choice do we really have? This is what people do to survive! No wonder so many Americans are sick and depressed and addicted to drugs! Well, I have news for you: it's not the only way! You've just been brainwashed into believing this is so.

One of the problems within any hierarchal structure is that we begin to relate to each other not as human beings, but as concepts. We have our mission statements, our budgets, our policy manuals, and our labels for everyone and everything, and these are placed above any individual human need. So if someone says, "Gosh, I feel stressed—I need a day off" or "My son is having a hard time right now and really needs me with him," the general response is, "According to our policy, you aren't due to get a day off for three more months until you've proven yourself."

Most corporations and government agencies in the United States are structured in such a way that those at the top are rarely held accountable for their insensitivity. This is done by ensuring that the work is compartmentalized. Each worker is only aware of his or her own role and often stripped of any decision-making authority. If we get pulled over by a police officer for driving too fast and explain that we didn't see the sign indicating the new speed limit, the cop tells us ignorance of the law is no excuse and writes us a ticket, stating, "I'm only doing my job." If customers complain about poor quality, lack of service, or that the bank charged them three hundred dollars in overdraft fees, they are told, sometimes even by someone with a manager's title, "I value you as a customer, but I can't do anything about that. My computer won't let me."

As a customer or citizen, we are purposely kept away from the person who could make a decision. But that person is hiding up above in a penthouse office, securely protected behind an army of human shields in the form of people desperate for a paycheck. These people didn't realize when they were signing up as "customer care" agents that they were really agreeing to accept the wrath of angry customers desperate not just to be heard, but also to be treated fairly.

### Your havingness in an organization is limited by its owners

No matter how talented, qualified, or motivated you are as an employee, no matter how well versed you are in the law of attraction, you will rarely be able to surpass the limits set by whoever heads the organizations you work for or belong to. This applies to your place of employment as well as to the educational and spiritual organizations you are affiliated with. These limits restrict how creative, innovative, independent, and successful you can be in your job. It doesn't matter if every ounce of your being is set on maximizing profits for the company; if the owner has lower havingness than you do or is in competition with your ability to create, you will not be able to be successful in the way you personally define success.

If your havingness exceeds that of the owner or those in charge, whether in terms of how much money or clients you can bring in, there are going to be problems. This is also true if you have a greater capacity for change, if you have a greater capacity for self-love and respect, and if you have more faith. These things will all be threatening to an employer who has less of them.

Sometimes when you first interview for a job or start with a company, it will seem as if the sky is the limit. Your boss may be successful, wealthy, and wise. However, it may turn out that your boss has reached his or her own ceiling and is not willing, out of fear or weariness, to push any further. You may have visions of taking the company into vast new arenas of possibility while the owner, director, or manager is simply focused on biding time until retirement. Sometimes you can tell where the parameters of success are set early on in the interview process by asking about the interviewer's or the company's top goals. A good question is: are they seeking to expand, or stay as they are? If you are a writer working with a publisher (or are seeking one), it's great to ask if that company is determined to send its titles to the bestseller lists or is merely satisfied with having a presence in the bookstores. The key here is to understand who you are dealing with, and respect their limitations while working toward eliminating your own.

## What happens when our heads
## rise up even past the steeple?

When we first take on a job or join an organization, we are usually fairly well matched with those we will be working with. However, over time our growth may be out of sync with the others.

Sometimes even when we belong to a spiritual organization, such as a church, we may find ourselves squished up under a ceiling of limitations that we will only be able to tolerate for so long. This can be quite painful when we've invested a lot of our time and energy in this organization, and particularly when we recognize that it's this very organization (or the people involved) that helped us to become who we are today.

In some cases, this organization or the person running it may have even saved our lives. Quite frequently as members of a church or school, we are much like children who grow up and then surpass their parents in terms of knowledge and skills. The difficult thing is that within our families we are usually expected to grow up and fly the coop, whereas within our churches, we are expected to grow up and continue to make contributions. When we realize we've outgrown the leaders or other members, we will often attempt at first to change the power dynamics or policies in order to make things more comfortable for ourselves. In some cases, this effort will be rewarded. We may even be given a promotion or gain status as a leader.

However, perhaps more frequently we will encounter the energy of resistance from those who are still at the stages we just outgrew. In some circumstances, they may feel so threatened by us that the only way to reestablish equilibrium within the group is to exile us, as quickly as possible. It's possible that we may find ourselves as outcasts before we are really emotionally ready to leave. To be viewed as a threat to the organization by those we dearly loved or respected can feel absolutely devastating. This has happened to members of countless churches. It happens in many metaphysical circles, as well as in secular groups.

### Can an organization suck out too much of our life force?

I think it's important to understand that anytime we are involved in corporate, nonprofit, religious, or spiritual organizations, we are donating some of our energy. This is true whether you are a full-time paid staff person, a volunteer, or just a member. This energy may be in the form of money, time, or parts of your spirit.

In my readings with a few people who were having severe financial problems for the first time in their lives, I got the image of their bodies being completely merged with a particular organization they were working or volunteering for. The next images that came to me reminded me of the Borg, that class of cyborgs in the *Star Trek* franchise whose minds are all linked together so they operate as a unit and are not allowed to be individuals. My clairvoyance was showing me that these organizations were like hungry machines that could only operate through the fuel they were sucking out of their members. It was a disturbing realization, to say the least! Now, this might not be a problem if the organization has lots of resources and is making great contributions to its individual members, but it appeared that in these cases, these organizations, which were of an educational and spiritual nature, were not doing financially well at all. Therefore the flow of abundance, rather than moving from the organization to its members, was flowing in the opposite direction, sucking them dry.

Whenever we work for anyone other than ourselves, we lend our creative life-force energy to others. What we get back in return are money and benefits. But what happens when our output of creative life-force energy is greater, much greater, than what we are actually getting back? We become depleted, and we feel bored, unsatisfied, taken advantage of, tired, sick, and our prosperity may suffer as well. Sound familiar?

The more involved we are, the more we merge energetically with the organization and its leaders and followers. This can enable us to grow, or it can stifle, repress, and weaken us. I mention this because no matter how lofty the goals, the vision, or the intentions of an organization's founders, we need to be aware that our relationship with this organization is not that much different from our relationships with individual people. Some of these are nurturing, and we nurture them and there is an equal exchange. Others appear to have our interests in mind (they had to reel us in in the first place) but are really sucking the life out of us. Sometimes we have strong agreements with these people and we really are fine with the dynamic, and then one day we wake up and discover the relationship no longer serves us in present time.

Leaving or being exiled from an organization, whether corporate or spiritual, can feel like a divorce or death, and often results in the same type of grieving period one goes through when losing a loved one. But there is always something else for us at the end of the tunnel. Quite often it's the discovery that we have what it takes to go into business for ourselves, or that we are the true masters we sought out when we joined the organization in the first place.

**Look out for multilevel marketing schemes**
There's a fine line between those who believe they have the power to manifest anything quickly and compulsive gamblers. There is no reason you should take extreme

risks with money you can't afford to lose just because you believe it will allow you to create more quickly.

There is an increasing trend to pair the concepts of the law of attraction with multilevel marketing schemes. In fact, several best-selling authors who have been leaders in the field of conscious creating are now marketing products for various multilevel marketing firms. What bothers me is that these "spiritual leaders" became successful by utilizing the law of attraction. Their successes really had nothing to do with the product they are selling. That is, until they used their established position of trust to convince people to buy the products! To me there is a lie in here somewhere. It creates confusion for those who are new to these concepts. They confuse the product for the methods that help to sell the product. They end up becoming cogs in a wheel of manipulation, of which they are only shown a couple of highly polished spokes. *In this way, the light is allowing itself to be used as the dark.*

I've had several friends who were involved in these schemes. A couple of them made a lot of money. Most of them sold a lot of product, irritated a lot of their friends, and in the end left the scheme feeling depleted, defeated, and confused about their ability to manifest. Those who do the best with these schemes usually already have access to a group of people who trust them and share similar spiritual ideals.

I've been to demonstrations where the presenter was in such an orgasmic frenzy over the effectiveness of a bottle of juice, you would have thought it was made from the blood of Jesus himself! This juice was not only going to free you from all pain, worry, and excess fat, but it was also going to save your soul—and you didn't need to do anything at all except drink three ounces a day, pay three hundred dollars a month, and convince all of your friends and family members to sign up as salespeople. Two weeks later I ran into one such presenter in a bathroom. She was screaming at her kid, had sores all over her face, and was popping amphetamines!

I mention this because what these pyramid schemes do is confuse boundaries between personal relationships. Those who are involved in the scheme must spend much of their energy making money for those at the top before they even see their own cut. Meanwhile, once they have expended a huge amount of life-force energy into the scheme, it becomes harder and harder to imagine quitting before seeing results. Those at the top will manipulate those below them into believing the problem isn't the product or the sales pitch, but rather their inability to correctly apply the law of attraction.

Regardless of whether or not the product does have useful qualities, those of us on the receiving end begin to wonder whether these people are talking to us because they like us or because they want to recruit us. I often think they themselves are not really sure either. A personal conversation with one of these marketers is never just a conversation, but a potential sales pitch. The more personal the conversation becomes, the easier it is to approach the subject, since the "product" has a helping component to it. In this way, the people at the top of the company pass their hungry tentacles down from person to person until the structure looks more like a skewer of bleeding hearts than a pyramid. I know these comments will upset some of my friends and readers, and I am sorry for that.

I suppose this is not that different from those unwitting people who pass around e-mails that share a meaningful story and then ask that the e-mail be passed on to five other people. These e-mails can really mean a lot to the person receiving them. But the recipients who forward them on generally don't realize these e-mails contain codes that allow the original sender to gain the e-mail addresses and other information for every person to whom the e-mail is sent. The companies that generate these e-mails do this so they can market products and even scams we would never knowingly agree to promote. I have friends and family to whom I've explained this over and over, and yet they still pass on these e-mails to me! It just sucks up too much time and energy as far as I am concerned.

The great prison we live in is the fear of
what others think of us.
—DAVID ICKE

# 16

# SELF-ESTEEM

In order to raise our self-esteem and feel better about ourselves, we have essentially two choices. We can:

1. Change ourselves so we match our picture of how we think we're supposed to be.

2. Change our picture of how and what we're supposed to be.

Sometimes changing ourselves is appropriate, sometimes it's not. Often, it's the changing or wanting to change ourselves to match that picture of perfection that causes us so much distress.

## Self-esteem = success,
## not the other way around!

From the thousands of clients and students I've worked with, I've learned that high self-esteem is one of the most essential ingredients for being able to manifest one's goals and ultimately the life one wishes to live. Self-esteem dictates how much you feel you deserve, how much you will ask for, and certainly how much you will strive for. It determines whether or not you will be able to communicate your needs, set boundaries with others, and enforce those boundaries. Success in so many endeavors—from starting your own business to excelling at a sport to developing your psychic or musical abilities—requires determination, focus, faith, confidence, skill, and communication and cooperation from others. Someone with low self-esteem is therefore going to have a hard time even starting to pursue these types of goals, much less excel at them.

To be successful in life, you must have a strong enough sense of yourself to be able stand up in a crowded room and say, "Pick me, I deserve it!" It doesn't really matter if others agree with this declaration. If you can't do this, someone else will. In case you haven't noticed, at any given time we have any number of people around us telling us why we can't achieve what we want to: because it's too hard, too expensive, will take too long, there are too many people already doing it, and blah blah blah blah blah.

Even those with nerves of steel can become discouraged by this silly chatter. (Heck, even after my third book contract, I still have occasional doubts as to whether or not I can even write.) But what about those already on shaky ground, who have been programmed with defeating messages since birth: that it's hopeless, it's not worth trying, that they are not good enough and never will be? If you don't have strong self-esteem, you aren't even going to allow yourself to consider the possibility of manifesting something that seems beyond the scope of what you've been told is possible for yourself.

When I first began teaching psychic skills, I noticed that the students in my classes who seemed to have the most difficulty accessing their psychic abilities were those whom I'd consider to have the lowest self-esteem in general. I found this fascinating. Part of it seemed to have to do with their preconceived ideas that they wouldn't do as well as everyone else. It wasn't that they weren't seeing images; it was that they doubted the validity or quality of the images they saw. It's easy to identify students with lower self-esteem right off the bat, because the first words out of their mouths are "I can't, I haven't, I don't." (Actually, they begin the majority of their sentences with these words!)

My students with lower self-esteem are harder on themselves, are constantly comparing themselves to the other students in the room (despite my instructions not to), and almost always come to the conclusion that they themselves are somehow inferior to everyone else. Quite often they aren't doing as well as the others—not because they don't have the inherent ability (usually it's clear in the first hour of class that they do), but because they give up and allow their attention to wander well before the other students do. Students suffering from lower self-esteem have even expressed concern that their lack of *perceived* progress or current emotional state may be inhibiting the rest of the group, which is never the case.

In my readings, a variety of common images arise for those struggling with self-love and trust. When such a client has a question about a relationship, I will sometimes see that client on hands and knees scrubbing the floor while his or her partner hovers above, pointing out the spot the client missed. This doesn't mean the client actually scrubs the floor, but you can be sure such clients expend a hundred times more energy pleasing their partner than the other way around. Another common image is that of a client looking in the mirror, but the mirror is very cloudy or cracked, or the client is breaking the mirror. Or someone else, sometimes many other people, are standing in the way of the client's ability to see his or her own image. This is pretty self-explanatory. I also will sometimes see my client sitting at a piano but barely touching the keys, or someone or several people playing the piano for my client. This means such a client is listening to others, as opposed to his or her own inner guidance.

## Some parts of ourselves
## have high self-esteem, some low

The problem with self-esteem is that it is not as clear-cut as many think it is. Some people actually have very high self-esteem in one area but very low self-esteem in another. Some people are confident in just about all areas except for one, and such people don't realize that low self-esteem is the culprit causing them to aim too low when it comes to choosing a partner or job. When I come across this situation in a reading, I will often see an image of the client with one very muscular arm and the other arm with a drooping muscle. This image is quite easy to work with, because I can first focus my attention on the strong arm to solicit information about the person's strengths, and then move to the other arm to request information about the client's area of weakness.

## Increasing self-esteem to attract relationships

One of the great things about both dream and clair-voyant (waking dream) images is that once you've noticed them, you can work with them to make changes and achieve desired results. Below I present meditations based on some of the symbols I've just discussed.

**Option 1:** Close your eyes. Ground yourself by connecting your lower body with a thick cord that shoots right down into the earth. This will keep you sturdy and help you release. Center yourself within your sixth chakra, behind your third eye, which you can imagine to be in the middle of your forehead. Pretend you are looking out of this chakra at a mirror that is about a foot in front of you. You can decorate this mirror with a border, and give it a base that connects into the earth. It is through this connection that you will be able to release whatever energy may come out of the mirror.

In the mirror, ask to see an image of yourself depicting the part of you that is strong and the part that is weak. Notice what appears. If there is any part of the image you feel is not optimal, then ask to see the color of the energy behind the part that is troublesome. Wait to see if you get a color, but if you don't, then just assign it a color and release the color down the base of the mirror. Continue to watch the image of yourself and notice if it changes now. If it doesn't, then imagine you are taking that entire image of yourself and releasing it down the base, or you can build a bonfire and toss the image of yourself (and anyone else who might pop up) into the fire. Don't worry: you aren't cremating yourself—just the former, outdated picture of yourself.

Now see yourself in the mirror exactly as you would like to see yourself. It's fine to get creative; go ahead and see yourself with huge muscles or any body feature you'd like. Make sure you see yourself with your head held high and a humongous smile on your face!

**Option 2:** Follow the instructions in the first paragraph of option 1.

Now, in the mirror, see an image of yourself sitting at a piano. Tell the image it is going to represent how clearly you are in communication with the innermost part of your heart, which is where your inner genie sleeps. You can start to visualize yourself playing the piano, and then see what happens next. Notice whether you actually do play or how you play, or if there is some kind of interference or if another person appears. Notice what happens to the piano.

**Option 3:** Follow the instructions in the first paragraph of option 1.

Look into the mirror in your imagination and visualize a pond or a very still lake. Notice the color of the water. This pond is going to represent your affinity for yourself. It's initially important to see the pond or lake as very still and peaceful (although if you can't, that's not a problem; it just reflects something going on within you). Watch this peaceful body of water for at least three minutes. If you get distracted, let whatever is distracting you flow right down your grounding cord.

Next, imagine you are approaching the pond. Look inside the pond and notice how your image appears. If you enjoy the image, then great. See yourself diving into the pond and notice whether or not the color of the pond changes. This color, if it feels good to you, will be the representation of the energy of self-affinity, and you can use it to heal yourself anytime by seeing it washing through your body from head to toe, and back up.

As you see an image of yourself gazing into the pond, if there is any part of the image you aren't happy with, then go ahead and completely drain the pond—and with it the undesirable image of yourself. Then ask the true color of your self-affinity to fill up the pond. Re-create an image of yourself in a happy, peaceful state, and visualize yourself frolicking in the colorful pond. Next put your attention on your actual physical body. You can even touch the top of your head with your hand. Then imagine taking the water from the pond and pouring it right into your physical head. Watch it flow from your head to your toes, over-flowing with the color of your new self-affinity.

## The hijacking of our hearts
## by corporate terrorists

Americans are under siege by terrorists and extortion-ists who never let themselves out of our sight for a moment. The true identities of these individuals are hidden behind the fortress of the corporation. They have already succeeded in hijacking our inner genies by convincing them to wish for what is in the cor-porations' best interests, not our own. There are far too many of these corporate terrorists to name, but just turn on your television set and you will see one of their ads convincing you that you have or will have a problem that only they can rectify. They have only two names for us: "sucker" and "consumer."

What are these things that we need and want so badly and that they are so eager to provide? They fall into two primary categories: the need to be loved and the need to be protected.

Many of you are thinking, "What? But I don't need protection! I can take care of myself—see, I'm all grown up." Oh, but are you? Can you? What if you are in a car accident? What if you get sick? What if some-one steals your identity? What if your house catches on fire? What if someone sues you? God forbid, what if the *Islamists* attack? What if your microwave breaks

SELF–ESTEEM    237

or your computer catches a virus or you lose your cell phone, or your hair or your mind or your erection? What if the absolutely unspeakable happens—besides losing that erection—and you gain weight, or the faintest hint of body odor escapes from the crevices of your shaven armpits? Or, do I dare suggest it, how could you possibly stand yourself if you came down with one more wrinkle (shudder) or (whisper) another varicose vein? I mean, who will want you then? What are the odds, the remotest chances, of ever finding, keeping, or having hugs, kisses, happiness, or success if you don't purchase protection from these insidious, disgusting horrors?

### How are the corporations so successful?

First of all, they get lawmakers on their side to enact legislation that not only protects their right to free speech (translation: the right to bombard you every waking hour with advertising), but that also actually criminalizes you for not purchasing their services (e.g., insurance) or penalizes you (e.g., the credit report) to the point that life's necessities become more and more difficult to obtain. They speak to you from every TV set, billboard, magazine, bus, park bench, and bumper sticker. Right now, these corporations are spending more time with your teenagers than you do, because they can be everywhere at once, while you cannot be.

The scary thing is they have succeeded in getting into our minds. How did we not see it coming? Every university across the country offers a marketing program, in which the emphasis is on training students to get into our heads through "branding" and advertising. They have branded you like a cow, and now they are between you and your reflection every time you glance in the mirror or in your partner's eyes. They have intercepted the communication between your spirit and your body, so now you no longer notice that your body is exhausted or hungry or broken.

### Disguising the means as the end

Here is the typical sequence of messages that have lured us in: "So, you want to buy a house? Well, forget about ever saving enough money—what you need is credit. What you need is a good credit rating. Don't have one? Really? Why? Is there something wrong with you? Well, never mind, all you need to do is sign up for a credit card or two, make as many purchases as possible, and pay your balance in full or on time each month. What? You're not sure you'll be able to do that? You're worried that something might come up: a lost job, lack of organization, an illness in the family that will get in the way of paying on time? Well, congratulations! You're exactly the kind of person we've been targeting! What? Maybe you don't want to buy a house after all? Well, don't you know that most landlords won't rent to someone who doesn't have great credit? You don't want to be homeless, do you?"

Now we are no longer solely focused on our goal of manifesting a great place to live, nor are we even focused on manifesting enough money for a great place to live. Instead, we are trying to obtain credit cards, trying to pay off our credit card bills, trying to prevent others from stealing our credit or from accusing us of an infraction that will show up on our credit report. Then there are those hundreds of thousands of people who fared well enough in the credit game to be "blessed" with variable interest rates, which are now ballooning so high that every ounce of these people's energy is going into saving their home from foreclosure.

And that is often not even the worst of it. The worst is the shame, the humiliation, the embarrassment, and the ignorance we feel as we compare ourselves to those around us who appear to be doing better than we are.

### Solutions

Okay, I think you get my point. Many of you are already becoming aware of how you are being duped. This awareness marks the first stage of reclaiming your power. The next stage is kicking these bastards out of our psyches, so we can remember who we are and what it is we really wanted in the first place. The next stage is replacing our self-loathing with love.

## Advocacy

Spread the word. Get the relevant advocacy organizations on board, as well as your political representatives, who as of this writing are not yet on board. It's really hard to understand how it's a crime to deny basic rights like shelter and employment based on skin color, age, and sexual orientation, but it's all right to deny people these things based on a credit-score number, a number that is largely formulated by the person's willingness to sign up for credit cards or lines of credit with huge interest rates and penalties.

If you are winning the game, then do what you can to support others who are not. Say no to more credit cards than are necessary. Evaluate people based on direct interactions with them and personal references. Understand that most people pay their rent before all other bills, and therefore strikes against them on their credit report for late payments do not reflect on their ability to be good tenants. Trust your intuition.

Take an economics course. Learn the language. Educate yourself before you get suckered in even more.

One day I went to my bank, Bank of America, because an Internet company had withdrawn money from my checking account without my authorization. I didn't have enough money in that account to cover this unauthorized withdrawal, and the bank charged me an overdraft fee that then snowballed into several others because I had written small checks prior to the withdrawal, which would have been covered had the one unauthorized withdrawal not been made. So now I was looking at close to two hundred and fifty dollars in overdraft fees.

I began explaining to the woman at the bank that I was in a bind, as my car had just broken down and I needed the money that had been taken out, both by this Internet company and then the bank, in order to fix my car and get to work. Guess what the banker's response was? "Do you own your own home?"

"No," I said, "I rent. What does that have to do with my checking account?"

"Oh, it doesn't," she replied, "but I was thinking if you needed money to pay for your car repairs and you owned a home, then you could just borrow against the equity in the house and use that money for your car and other bills."

I looked at her like she was nuts. "Do you really think that would be a wise thing to do even if I did own a house with equity in it?" I asked.

"Well," she said with a sickeningly sweet smile, "you do need a way to get to work, don't you?"

### For those of you who are not faring well

The question always boils down to this: do you keep playing, and risk losing everything because you don't have the resources to play, or do you drop out of the game? Dropping out would mean you no longer care what your credit report looks like, and you no longer answer calls from creditors unless foreclosure agents or the IRS is calling. (In such cases, you need to make some choices fast, consult with professionals, and be on top of it all. It's better to give your possessions back to the bank, or sell what you can as early as possible, instead of waiting for someone to take them away.)

If you choose not to play, then you need to believe that you will be able to manifest all you need by attracting people into your life who are willing to see you as a human being as opposed to a number or a trophy. I don't care which course of action you choose. My main concern is that you understand you are worth more than your credit score—you are worth more than that number on the scale—and that whether you are looking for a husband or a wife, a home to live in, a great job, or a contract for your creative project, there is someone out there, lots of *someones*, even more desperate to find you!

Recently I came across an article from the *Washington Post*, written by Alec Klein and entitled "Credit Raters' Power Leads to Abuses." The article starts out describing how Moody's Investors Service was aggressively courting Hannover Re, one of the largest insurance companies in Germany. Hannover was already paying other companies to rate its services and didn't see why it should pay for Moody's. The following is an excerpt from the article:

*Moody's began evaluating Hannover anyway, giving it weaker marks over successive years and publishing the results while seeking Hannover's business. Still, the insurer refused to pay. Then last year, even as other credit raters continued to give Hannover a clean bill of health, Moody's cut Hannover's debt to junk status. Shareholders worldwide, alarmed by the downgrade, dumped the insurer's stock, lowering its market value by about $175 million within hours.*

*What happened to Hannover begins to explain why many corporations, municipalities, and foreign governments have grown wary of the big three credit-rating companies . . . as they have expanded into global powers without formal oversight.*

*The rating companies are free to set their own rules and practices, which sometimes leads to abuse, according to many people inside and outside of the industry . . . In [some] cases, the credit raters have strong-armed clients by threatening to withdraw their ratings—a move that can raise a borrower's interest payments.*

I include this article excerpt here to help you understand that it's not just the little people who have been strong-armed by the system, but also small and large companies alike. If this is news to you, don't be surprised. I am writing about this here because I haven't heard a single person echo my disgust over this weapon called the credit report, which is being used not just against the American people but also against citizens and businesses throughout the world. If a rating company has the power and the audacity to alter a single number that leads to the loss of $175 million in hours for a major company, why on earth would it care about your own well-being?

The crime isn't just occurring because of these crooks; it's happening because our government has been refusing to do anything about them. These financiers are apparently above all laws, while you are paying penalties or fearful of receiving fines every time you drive your car, park your car, pay your taxes, et cetera, et cetera, et cetera.

### EXERCISE
## Paid in full

See yourself paying off your creditors and having a piece of paper that reads "Paid in full." You can even write a check for the full amount, tape it to your wall, and bless it whenever you happen to notice it. What this does is help you pay on an energetic level for the physical level to follow, while helping you know psychologically that you are doing your best and that everything will be easily and effortlessly manifested in the physical soon afterward.

Get out a piece of paper, and write down the following petition:

*Dear God: Please intervene and help end my debts. Help me either to pay them in a timely, easy manner that will only positively impact my life, or have them forgiven completely. I ask that you help me release the guilt I feel and create opportunities in my life that will be lucrative and fulfilling. I ask for complete forgiveness for all of my past behavior regarding my finances, and I ask that you give me the strength, fortitude, knowledge, and understanding to make the best decisions that will help me live my life debt free and guilt free. I thank you for releasing me from these debts and burdens. I thank you for bringing abundance, prosperity, and love to anyone to whom I have ever owed money. Thank you for infusing my life with blessed forgiveness. Sincerely, [your name].*

Then make a list of all the people you can possibly think of who would support you in this petition. List them as co-signers to your petition, so you can see how supported you really are. These can be real people or fictional people. Then go take a nap, a walk, or a bath, or do some other nice thing for yourself.

They lend people money that doesn't exist and
charge them interest . . . and we stand for that.
—DAVID ICKE
Boredom is the root of all evil—the despairing refusal to be oneself.
—SØREN KIERKEGAARD
The significant problems we face cannot be solved at the same level
of thinking we were at when we created them.
—ALBERT EINSTEIN

# 17

# THE STATE OF THE WORLD
# IS NOT THE WORLD

The challenge we face as conscious creators is this:

On the one hand, we know that we can create our
own personal realities. Many of us have even figured
out how to structure much of our days so we are doing
what we love, with those we love, in places that we
love. Everything is just fine and dandy, until we turn
on our television sets and see people being blown apart
in Iraq, or losing their homes to predatory lenders. We
may be feeling on top of the world until we stop for
gas and discover it's gone up another fifty cents, or we

run into the grocery store to buy a five-dollar loaf of white bread, or we are pulled over by the motorcycle cop who writes us a ticket for failing to wear a shoulder strap or for parking a quarter-inch too far from the curb or for picking our noses at an undesignated stop. Suddenly, we understand why some people go postal.

So how on earth do we keep our inner state of peace, when it feels like there are pressures from everywhere around us that want to take that state of peace away from us?

Do we just think positively and ignore everything that's bothering us?

Do we just manifest more money to pay for the ever-increasing expenses around us?

Do we just walk or drive the straight and narrow line, praying that we don't do anything wrong that will pull us into the web of the tax-collecting police state?

If misfortune does come our way, do we just pay up and move on without resistance?

Do we choose to downsize, restructure, and let go, so that we have less stress, fewer expenses, and fewer people and things to deal with?

Do we just tune out the world, turn off our television sets, and focus on our own personal lives?

**Our picture of the world is not the world**
Over the course of the last nine months, I have rewritten this chapter no less than twenty times. I've finally

figured out there are three reasons why. One, I have not been very neutral about the state of the world. Two, my view of the state of the world keeps changing as does the world itself. And three, whose world exactly are we talking about here?

My original goal in writing this chapter was to address the confusion plaguing most people, and particularly those on the path of conscious creation. I wanted to bring awareness to all Americans who are beating themselves up for their failure to obtain or hold on to the "American dream," in which the ideas of home ownership and the ability to pay one's bills are intricately linked. I wanted to demonstrate that one's perceived failings are not strictly due to one's own financial mismanagement, but that we have been set up for failure from the start. I wanted to demonstrate that the credit report is a dangerous tool by which the financial institutions extort money from us and lure us into financial slavery—and that we as Americans have become nothing more than pawns in a complex game, masterminded by those in a class so far removed and shielded from the rest of the players that most of us are not even aware of their existence. While the methods have been complex, the plot has been pretty simple: the puppeteers get the dough, and the rest of us get the bill or pay the price.

I was really beginning to feel like the only woman they hadn't yet gotten in *Invasion of the Body Snatchers*!

I wasn't sure if I'd be able to pull out enough Americans from their pods of mind control fast enough before I myself became too weary and drifted off into sleep like the rest of them.

When I first began this chapter, I was angry and feeling victimized. I would run through my laundry list of complaints, aware that all I was doing was ranting and wasting time but unable to stop myself. I saw my deadline for the entire book approach and pass me by like a lone trucker on a desert highway, oblivious to a lost hitchhiker wandering aimlessly in circles in the harshness of the night.

Not surprisingly, my computer crashed and I lost most of this chapter. I had a full-service warranty on my computer from CompUSA, but a month after selling me the expensive service plan, they closed all their local stores (as if they didn't suspect this was going to happen when they sold me the in-store service plan). I was told my only option was to mail my precious writing tool to an address somewhere far across the country, and wait. This was highly frustrating for me, since I had also wiped my schedule clean of appointments to make more progress on this book, but I also knew it was a blessing in disguise. I needed to take a break. I realized I hadn't been running my energy.

### Running energy
*Running energy* is a form of meditation that helps to distance you from the pictures you are stuck in. It is like giving the inside of your body and your aura a psychic shower. It's a process by which you visualize colored light or water rushing through every part of your body. This visualization is a type of meditation that speeds up the process of letting go of the pictures that control and limit your perceptions and ultimately your creations. (I discuss running energy in greater detail in my first two books.)

After thirty refreshing minutes of running my energy, I understood what was wrong with this chapter. I realized my writing was filled with pain and feelings of rejection, guilt, and shame for not having met other people's definitions of success. Sure, I wanted to help, but I was also trying to change others' views so they would stop judging me. I knew that my angry rants weren't going to lift me or anyone else up, but rather they would create more of the same. So I went back to the basics, and I looked back to the main tenets of the law of attraction, outlined in chapter 2:

- Your thoughts and feelings magnetize situations, objects, and people to you
- Positivity breeds positivity, negativity attracts negativity

- By raising your vibrational frequency, you attract things more quickly to yourself
- Your underlying, unconscious feelings and programming can influence your manifestations

When I read these over, it was clear that both I and most of the conscious creators I knew were forgetting to apply these tenets to whatever we deemed as the "outside world." Why was this, I wondered? Why the strong split?

It seems to me that part of the problem lies in the distinction we make between that which falls under our definition of our personal life and that which belongs to the "outside world." This distinction is based on a variety of considerations and perceptions, many of which are unconscious. They include the following:

- How many of the events revolve around us— are we the main protagonists or the viewers?
- How much control we have over events and situations
- How close we are to these events in physical distance
- How much of the whole picture can we see
- How much the events affect our moment-to-moment enjoyment of our lives
- How obvious is it that we are impacted by events
- Whether we observe events firsthand or through secondary sources such as the media

When it comes to that which we define as part of our "personal lives," we are the stars and main protagonists. We see, or think we see, more of the whole picture because we experience events firsthand; they happen to us, and therefore we feel we have more control over them. They are a part of us. That which we think of as the "outside world" contains events that we mostly experience through secondary sources, usually through the media or via communications with friends and teachers who share their pictures of the world with us. Therefore we aren't as certain about our relationship to these events, and we don't feel we have the same level of understanding or control over them, because they seem to encompass so much more than our personal lives do. Because we feel we have less control, we forget that we can also apply the law of attraction to this world outside ourselves.

### The news

Our choice of news programs is as limited as our choice of political representatives! We are not a truly democratic society, but rather a society that romanticizes the myths and ideals of democracy.

The media is the window that allows us to see past our little homes into other parts of the world. However, we still need to remember that we only see tiny slices of the outside world, and these slices are chosen by others with agendas that cause them to want to tell very specific stories.

If you walk into any movie-rental store, you will see it is divided into sections based on topics. In the family section you will find charming cartoons about rainbows and unicorns and puppy dogs saving the day. In the horror section you will find gory tales of mutilation and bloodshed. The nice thing about renting movies is that you get to choose not only what kind of story you are going to watch, but also what type of experience you are going to participate in. The children's story may make you laugh and bring back your own fanciful dreams, or it might bore you. On the other hand, that horror movie is going to get your adrenaline going; it's going to scare you, and it's going to make you wonder what that noise was outside and whether or not you really are safe. It may even impact how well you sleep tonight or thirty years from now. Both of these have the capacity to change your pictures of the world and thus the world itself. If we scare ourselves enough, we might begin to think the world is a scary place, and our life force may turn toward seeking protection or retaliation.

When it comes to the news projected on our television sets, we have far fewer options. The news is about whatever the producers and writers choose for us. We turn on our TV sets, open our newspapers, even sign onto our e-mail, and there it is: what someone else has chosen. There are very few news programs that just focus on loving acts of kindness. Instead, we get the horror and the killing and the ugliness. Unlike the films we rent, the news is supposed to be real. This means there really is a bogeyman out there and he might really get you. This content is often as biased as that of any fictional horror flick, in which the choice of scenes and shots is carefully orchestrated by its creators.

Take the news coverage of the Iraq war, for instance. News programs can show us a casket of an American soldier, or they can show us a smiling Iraqi boy holding an American flag. We are flashed this image for a moment, and now we hold an idea in our minds that leads to our opinions and overall belief system about the war and the state of the world—even though the war and the world are made up of trillions upon trillions of individual flashes and images and truths. In this way, others are choosing and manipulating our pictures of reality for us based on their own positions and economic interests.

Do you ever wonder why we put up with this? What do you think people would do if the owner of their favorite video store decided that the only films she was going to make available were the horror films? Many of us would stop going to that store. Right? But what if every other store followed suit? I suspect, over time, if this were the only option for this type of entertainment, that we might eventually return to that store, telling ourselves, well, we can always close our eyes for the really icky parts. After even more time, we might actually forget that any other kind of film ever existed, or we might begin to redefine the icky parts as a normal, unavoidable aspect of life.

This might seem far-fetched, but it's not. This is actually what is starting to happen. The horror sections of these stores are expanding. Meanwhile, if you ask any agents or managers of child actors, they will tell you there are fewer and fewer projects for kids these days. Why? Because there are fewer television shows for and about kids. They've been replaced with shows like *Dexter*, the main character of which is deemed "America's most beloved serial killer"; or *Californication*, about, well, need I say more; or *Nip/Tuck*, which is about a group of plastic surgeons who molest and take advantage of the women they cut open.

Getting back to our view of the world, it is very much colored by the images and information others have chosen for us. These others are not necessarily on the same path we are on. So, now we are confused. We have these images swirling around in our heads. We begin thinking things are bad. Worse than bad. So bad that we can't even allow our children to play outside anymore.

If you grew up in a family where your parents were abusive and everyone put each other down and life was difficult, and you live in a neighborhood where everyone is killing each other and you risk your life even to go to school, how could you possibly think there was anything else other than that for you? You wouldn't. And therefore you won't strive for anything else, because what else is there to strive for? This is what is happening in our inner cities, and this is what happens in every area of our globe that is warring or poverty-stricken.

In many "developing" nations, the ambition of millions of people is to get out and go to America. Such folks are convinced that their countries and their lives there will never improve, and therefore they don't strive to make their countries better. Instead, they put all their life-force energy into getting out, and as a result their own countries further atrophy.

In America we have hope; that is what has made our country strong. However, in the past decade many of us have begun to realize that the freedoms and privileges we enjoyed have grossly eroded. Since the attacks on the World Trade Center and the Pentagon on September 11, 2001, we have been handed fear pictures and told through overt statements and covert manipulation that we must hand over our freedoms in exchange for protection. This process is no different from the one that happens to us as children, when our parents hand us pictures that say, "You are not strong enough to take care of yourself" or "You are not smart enough to become a doctor" or "You are not pretty enough to get a great man, so just settle for less." After a while we accept these pictures into our souls, and they become magnets that draw corresponding experiences.

Fortunately, most of us don't experience these pictures directly, but instead do so vicariously through our television sets. However, even from the safe distance of our living rooms we experience the emotional pain. This pain weakens the power of our inner genie by lowering her vibration, and therefore makes it much more difficult for us to manifest on a personal level. The question then is: why do we allow this process to happen?

## We still want someone to take care of us

There is a reason why the majority of Americans have so little awareness, understanding, and perspective about topics that impact them on a minute-to-minute basis. These topics include economics, finance, history, and even parapsychology and creativity. Responsibility for this can't be placed solely on those who benefit from this ignorance. We complain about the educational system for our children, but what are we doing to educate ourselves as adults? So what if someone already handed us a diploma and told us we were done. Aren't we mature enough to pick up some books or enroll in some basic classes that teach us how to calculate a variable interest rate or understand the implications of, and differences between, prime and subprime lending?

There are some incredibly innovative and thorough authors who are attempting to provide such education. Howard Zinn has written *A People's History of the United States*. Howard Bloom has written *Reinventing Capitalism: Putting Soul in the Machine*, which he calls a "radical reperception of western civilization," as well as the earlier *Global Brain: The Evolution of Mass Mind from the Big Bang to the 21st Century*. Dean Radin's books *The Conscious Universe* and *Entangled Minds* present thousands of pages of solid research that suggests the majority of us who have intuitive and precognitive experiences are not crazy or unusual after all.

I believe most of us have a deep longing and need to feel we are being cared for by someone who seems to have more answers than we do. Researchers have clearly demonstrated that children need structure and supervision. They don't do well with parents who are overly strict, but they also don't do well with parents who are overly permissive. It's clear that most kids like to have the freedom to make their own choices—until they are confused, hungry, or overwhelmed, and then they appreciate it very much when Mommy or Daddy tells them it's time to turn out the lights. Adults are no different. We have replaced our moms and dads with our politicians, bankers, stockbrokers, and news anchors. Are these really the people we want tucking us in at night? But they are so happy to do it!

I believe that our need to be led and protected is now attracting leaders who are far too authoritarian. Our government and its enforcers are taking a far too strict approach. The police used to hand out warnings. Now they give you a three-hundred-dollar ticket and tell you to duke it out with the judge. So you are guaranteed to lose at least half a day in court regardless of whether you are "guilty" or not. Andy Griffith has turned into RoboCop!

However, I suspect that we will not be impacted by this tightening of controls unless we are already struggling with something within ourselves that mirrors this oppression. In my own case, I've just recently become aware of the relentless pressure and control I exert on myself to keep performing and achieving no matter how depleted I am (as evidenced by the fact that it's well past midnight and I'm still plugging along here). Is it any wonder that I have been bumping up against those who don't want to give me a break either? Still, this awareness didn't stop me from writing to the mayor and all the city-council members of my city, Moorpark, to complain after a cop wrote me a ticket for driving with my headlights off when I had only just left a lighted parking lot seconds before.

# Judgment

Just as all opportunities are created by people, so are all problems. A problem is not a tangible thing. It's a situation that we are judging. It's a negative definition of a particular experience for which we lack perspective. As humans, most of us spend our days distinguishing between whether something or someone is good or bad, right or wrong, honorable or dishonorable. We have learned to view ourselves, each other, and the state of the world through the filters of blame and judgment. This judgment creates a wedge between our own heart and mind and our spirit and body. It creates a barricade between ourselves and anyone we deem as remotely different from us in appearance, behavior, attitude, and ethics. It cuts us off from that which created us, that which can heal us, and the wellspring of creativity that is supposed to be our birthright.

When we judge someone or something, we have sidetracked ourselves from creative solutions. I am sure you've noticed how the moment a perceived injustice happens, a battle cry goes out for retribution. Nothing can happen anymore without someone else being responsible or made to pay. We try to solve our pain by finding someone, anyone, to dump the blame on, with the idea that if this other person suffers or hands over their money, our own suffering will somehow be alleviated. All of our wars and our social problems can be linked to judgment and our unconscious projections upon our enemies. We try to solve our pain by judging others, but this just creates more pain.

### The opposite of blame is appreciation
While my computer was down, I spent a lot of time meditating and applying the techniques offered in this book to my goals for what I define as the "state of the world" and my perceptions of it, and some interesting things began to happen.

It's been said already, but appreciating what we have really does put things into proper perspective, because it brings us into the present moment, which, as Eckhart Tolle reminds us and reminds us and reminds us, is all there is. (We really do need the reminding!) Appreciation is perhaps the highest energy you can run, after laughter and lightheartedness.

Of course, my usual response at the gas pump when the prices go up is to look around to see who else is within earshot, and then let out an exasperated, "Can you believe what they're doing to us?!" I usually get either an adamant nodding of heads, a chuckle, or a startled look that says, "Who is this weirdo?" But one morning, after visualizing the world as I desired it to be, I had a different response. It began with the thought, *Wow, I'm really fortunate in this moment even to have gas at all! I am fortunate to have a car that runs, to have a driver's license, even to know how to drive! I am blessed to have a foot that can step on the gas pedal and hands that can direct the steering wheel. I am so incredibly blessed to have gas money, even money for the cup of coffee I am about to purchase that I don't really need at all.*

On that morning, for perhaps the first time in over a year, I drove away from the pump feeling lucky instead of victimized.

### Are we really being harmed by the things that upset us the most?

Once I began appreciating the fact that I did in fact have money for gas, even at four dollars per gallon, I wondered why it was that I was complaining about the high prices so much. I began asking myself, "In this very moment, is my life really being influenced by global warming or the national debt, or am I just getting upset over the ideas of these things?" The fact was, in this moment, on a personal level, I had more freedom in terms of my time schedule, and more clients, more love, and more prosperity than I had ever had in my life.

Now you try it. Choose anything that is getting your blood boiling about the state of the world. Let's take the price of gas, for example. Ask yourself, "Did the price of gas today really stop me from going somewhere?" Now, it may very well have impacted your decision of whether or not to take a trip. However, if you are really honest with yourself, you will most likely find that the price of gas did not make it impossible for you to do something that you truly needed to do or go somewhere you wanted to go.

For myself, I had a harder time coming up with gas money in the late 1980s, when for a while gas was under eighty cents per gallon, than I did in the summer of 2008, when it was close to five dollars per gallon. Back in the 1980s, I shared a car with my twin sister. We were always broke, so most of the time I'd put a dollar or two of gas in our Chevy Malibu, and then she'd drive the car or vice versa; one of us was running out of gas at least once a week. Yet I haven't run out of gas since it first went up to two dollars per gallon!

The reality is that many of us are finding ways to manifest money to accommodate these higher prices, or are choosing alternatives such as taking public transportation or riding our bikes, which is getting us into better shape. Sometimes the price of gas is a convenient excuse for not having to go somewhere. It lets us off the hook. So maybe the price of gas is presenting an opportunity for Americans to do things differently, which will ultimately serve us all. Or maybe it just sucks. You don't have to choose between these possibilities; both may be true. The point here is that if we get out of resistance to what is before us—the higher prices—then we can remain or come back to a place of calmness and sanity. This is a much stronger position from which to effect change.

Oh, there's one more thing I thought I'd mention. Just a few weeks after I released all those negative feelings about the high gas prices, the price of gas started dropping; after several weeks, it had dropped in half—and it's remained there ever since! Some people say it's a matter of time before the price of gas goes back up. I say that if enough of us believe it won't (or do something to ensure it won't), then perhaps it will drop even more, or perhaps the need for gasoline will become obsolete.

## Don't fall into the trap of believing in the status quo!

It's important for you to get this: *you can have more abundance in a recession or depression than you've ever had!*

- You can have peace, happiness, and success in a time when most people seem to be going bonkers.
- In the midst of global warming or even a global financial conspiracy, you can enjoy the sun and the earth as the magnificent things they are. We need the sun as much as we need the plants, no matter what the manufacturers of toxic sunscreen products want us to believe.

## Healing the pain of the victim citizen

It's time to unleash our inner genies on the level of global/world peace!

1. Sit in a chair. Relax.

2. Acknowledge your anger, frustration, or fear. After an initial minute of contemplation, bring yourself to a feeling place rather than one of thinking. Don't judge or blame yourself, just let yourself feel the emotion. Ask yourself where in your body you feel these unpleasant feelings. Put your hand over that part, and breathe. Bring your spirit, your attention, and your focus to that part. Allow yourself to be fully in that location. Immerse yourself in the feeling. Feeling is the key here. Breathe. The feeling might get really strong for a moment. Just sit there with it until it starts to intensify. Breathe through it and let it go.

3. Hold out your hands. Imagine you are taking all your feelings—the hurt, the anger, the helplessness—and rolling them up in a big ball. At this point you might start to feel pain in or around certain body parts. Imagine you are holding this red energy ball over wherever your body feels the pain or tightness. Hold the ball in your hands.

4. Do the God as a magic symbol exercise from chapter 13. Be God for a moment and have the

light of God shining through you. Hold this red ball of hurt and allow the white light of God to wash through it, dissolving it or transforming it—and then release the ball, sending it up to the heavens, into the ocean, or deep within the earth.

5. Create a symbol that represents your hope for the world. Take this symbol and hang it up on your wall. Gaze at it each day and pray to it that it helps you along your path of healing, acceptance, and right action. Draw the symbol on a piece of paper and stick it in your purse or wallet, or hang it in your car or on your mirror. Know that this is your own private symbol. It doesn't matter if everyone else around you is hopeless or talking about the end times. This symbol will help you keep a positive frame of mind. Until there is no world left at all, there is no good reason to give up the hope that things will get gloriously better.

6. Identify one thing wrong with the world or your country right now. Then choose to do something creative to combat this: it might be your own project, or it might be jumping aboard one that someone else has begun.

Please note that every single exercise in this book can be used for manifesting the qualities and attributes that you'd like to see in the world, in your country, in your hometown, in your home, and in your personal life!

### Reasons to manifest disaster

Within a short time of doing the above exercise, I discovered that my attitude about the state of the world was changing. The day I realized this, my computer was returned to me, seemingly better than ever. However, I found it difficult to get back to writing, because there was a much more compelling drama playing out on the television set. Hurricane Gustav was on its way, and close to three million people were evacuating from the same regions of Louisiana that had been so ravaged by flooding just three years before during Hurricane Katrina. Of course the sun was shining where I was in California, but that didn't stop me from racing from channel to channel, watching this new drama unfold. Its ending was relatively anticlimactic, as the hurricane took a detour and spared New Orleans and its people.

However, the sequel took just over a week to arrive, when Hurricane Ike came charging toward the Texas coast, prompting the National Weather Service to broadcast the most ominous warning it had ever issued, one that seemed to startle even the most seasoned news anchors. The message, in summary, was, "People living anywhere near Galveston, Texas, get out while you can. If you stay, you will be facing certain and imminent death." The warnings were correct. Galveston was pulverized, and even the city of Houston, forty-five miles inland, was severely affected, with billions of dollars in damage to skyscrapers and homes, and millions of people without electricity or water for up to several weeks.

Now, these events had nothing to do with me. I didn't even know anyone in the area, but I could hardly bring myself to do anything but watch it all come down on the tube. Why? Because I wanted to see what would happen next, and it was far more interesting than what was happening in my life at the time.

Contrast this with where I was on September 11, 2001, when airplanes crashed into the World Trade Center and the Pentagon. I had just started film school. I didn't even own a television set. I was scheduled to direct my first short film that very morning. When my sister called and left me a voicemail telling me I needed to get to a television set because something really bad was happening, I didn't consider canceling my plans for a second. Sure, I was concerned; my brother and his wife lived in Brooklyn. But I knew there was nothing I could do from Arizona. I was so excited about my film and all I was learning. When a couple of actors called to say they wouldn't be coming in that day because the events back east were just too disturbing, at first I was confused. "Do you have family there?" I asked.

"No," they said.

"Oh, well, are you going there to help out?" I asked.

"No," they responded.

"Well, is there anything you can do from your living room other than feel bad and scared?"

"No," they said, "but it wouldn't feel right to be doing something as frivolous as acting on a day like today, would it?" Each of the actors spoke to me with growing irritation and distress.

"Don't you love acting?" I asked them. "Wouldn't this be a better energy to run, for yourself and the country? The terrorists want us to feel afraid. Are you going to give them what they want? It's your choice."

One of them agreed, showed up, and had a great time, later landing other roles as a result of being in this little film. The other did not show up. While I had sympathy and understanding for the events of that tragic day, I actually did not see any footage of the attacks for almost six months afterward. Meanwhile, during those six months I had the most creative time of my life and made some films that since then seem to have had an uplifting effect on others. This was not the response the terrorists wanted. Ironically, it was not the response many of my fellow Americans wanted either, as evidenced by their judgment toward me.

However, on the day of the Galveston hurricane, almost exactly seven years to the day after the attacks of 9/11, I was at home, watching TV, depressed about not knowing which direction to go with this chapter, and feeling bored. I believe that most Americans are bored, even the ones who are busy 24/7. Boredom has less to do with being busy and more to do with passion and fulfillment. In my own life, early on, I recognized that when I was feeling bored, trouble would soon find its way to my door. I believe that, deep down, a part of too many of us longs for the drama and accompanying adrenaline rush that is experienced in the midst of the massive storms and earth changes that we are either beginning to see or are prophesied to be near.

Apart from the drama, many folks long for a complete overhaul of life as they know it. Some people can't stomach the idea that life will be the same ole same ole for the next thirty, forty, or sixty years, but they lack the gumption or know-how required to make their own personal life more satisfying. Others are so disgusted and dismayed by the existing power structures within society that they long for a change that will bring them into balance or completely flip them. They see no other way except for absolute destruction.

To be successful in America, a certain skill set is required that might be quite different if all hell broke loose. There is little place in our society for men with physical strength and prowess to shine, except in the arenas of sports or war. But send the earth into a big enough tailspin, and these are exactly the guys who will be needed to protect and rebuild our communities.

If the price of gas rockets so high, or the supply runs so low, that people can no longer drive their vehicles, then the traditional nine-to-five grind of a workday will need to shift. While I do believe that the workplace, with its regimented schedule, is in the process of changing, I don't believe it's going to happen from lack of fuel, since the moment the companies who were profiting from the sale of oil are no longer profiting, they will quickly develop new fuel or transportation sources to reseed their bank accounts. Instead, I believe this change is coming because of a shift in consciousness, which will be precipitated by enough people raising their energetic frequencies through self-healing and gaining control of their emotional states, so they realize there is another way.

Those of you from the Midwest or the East Coast surely remember wintry days as a child, when you wished for a big snowstorm so you could stay home from school. Instead of waiting for a snowstorm, why didn't you just go to your teachers and parents and say, "I really need a day off school. I'm getting bored. I want to do something else today."

Why? Because they would have looked at you like you were nuts, dumb, or both, and said, "Yeah, right. So would I."

As adults, most of us still are in the same position, petrified to take a day off unless someone else gives us permission. From our very first day on the job, we agree to relinquish our personal freedom for eight or more hours a day. We agree to ignore the needs of our body and the yearnings of our heart in exchange for seven or seventeen bucks an hour. We leave our personality, our spirit, and our true self locked away in the hot car all day where they shrivel and cry out for us. But we've rolled up the windows, turned up the stereo, and turned our backs to their muffled screams until they fade into nothing more than a nagging itch suggesting that at some point, somewhere, we left something behind that might have mattered.

So the weather or any natural disaster is a convenient excuse to let us off the hook without us having to be personally accountable. Perhaps when the Big One comes, there won't be any office to return to.

The key here is to tune in to where are we looking for sources outside ourselves to do for us what we are unwilling or feeling unable to do for ourselves. When we are pushing away our need for change, creativity, or control in our own lives, that is when our manifestations become unhealthy and dangerous.

With the storms over, I was ready to get back to this chapter. However, it seemed as if every time I went to write, no matter how much I promised myself I would not let myself get distracted, the one phone call, e-mail, bill, or knock on the door would come that just had to be dealt with, or so it seemed.

### Technology and stress

We have obviously been in the midst of a technological revolution-evolution for the past century, one that's grown exponentially in the past decade. Our technology has opened up many new avenues for self-expression, creativity, communication, and new ways of doing business and earning income—not just for adults, but for our children as well. In fact, it's the kids who are faring better than the adults. They are having an easier time understanding how to work this technology, because they have developed along with it. Teens also have more time or make the time to enjoy this technology, while adults are having to learn how it all works in order to meet the survival needs of themselves and their teens (which might include weekly trips to the electronics store!).

That being said, the attention spans of our children and teens are decreasing. They are used to constant sensory stimulation and flitting from one source of entertainment to the next; kids will wander around in circles, not sure what to do with themselves, when made to part with their technology. My own son automatically picks up a remote control whenever he passes by the television set. I used to reprimand him for this, since he does it even after we agree he has something else to do. However, now I understand it's automatic. The second something moving catches our children's attention, they are absorbed in it. We as parents complain, but how are we any different when the second our cell phone rings, a text message beeps, or an e-mail pops up, we jump on it as if the survival of the entire universe rested solely on answering it? While our inability to focus on any one thing certainly doesn't seem like a positive, only time will tell if we aren't actually being prepared for a future that might require this skill.

### Increase in expenses
The challenge is that much of this technology zaps up our time and energy and costs money, way more money than we had to pay in the past for household expenses. In the good ole days, it used to be that we had to pay for rent or the mortgage if there was one, a phone bill, and a few utility bills. Now we pay for cable television, computers, software, printers, Internet connections, possibly websites or newsletters if we are trying to market just about anything, and cell phones in addition to land lines, because our cell phones are not always reliable. All of that is on top of whatever costs we have for owning a car and of course the multitudes of types of insurance and licenses we must pay for, or the fines we incur for not having them. Whether or not our income has gone up, we obviously have a lot more to deal with.

The explosion of technology has resulted in an abundance of new avenues for communication. The number of people we come into contact with, albeit virtually, has therefore drastically increased. This is true of not just acquaintances and business contacts (whom we may meet on MySpace or Facebook, or in chat rooms) but of our intimate relationships as well. With a wider pool of possible mates and a lessening of the taboos on divorce, so many of us have our current significant other and our "no-longer-that-significant other," as well as their children, to support and contend with.

The positive side is we never have to be lonely, because we can connect with those with similar interests in a heartbeat, and we can constantly reinvent ourselves and our lives like never before. And if we have a question about absolutely anything, all we have to do is Google it and we will have immediate answers. What could be more exciting than that?

The downside is that we are handling so many more wishes and wants and needs than ever before from other people, as well as our own, and many of us feel as though we're nearing our breaking point. It's as if we have too many options, too many choices, too many questions and even answers, too many people, too many bills, too many responsibilities—heck, even too many books to read . . . or write! Meanwhile, there are still just twenty-four hours in a day and just one of each of us.

As I write this, I get an image of two feet standing on opposite shores. One shore is farther away and belongs to the world called *when life was simpler*. The closer shore belongs to the world called *today*. Most children live in the world of today. However, most adults over the age of forty are struggling to balance themselves between these two worlds. The trouble is, the worlds are moving farther away from each other at a faster rate. Our legs can only stretch so far before we must choose which world we are going to belong to. This is why we have the sensation of being overwhelmed, of being "stretched too thin." If we don't make a conscious choice soon, we may be pulled in half.

To choose the old world means giving up most of this cool stuff and living in places where there are others still living more simply, such as the wilderness of Alaska or the Appalachian Mountains or the beaches of Bora Bora. Ironically, these places are being threatened by those who constantly need to find new sources of energy to feed the insatiable appetite of the world of today.

To succeed in the world of today means first, we as individual citizens are going to have get out of resistance to these changes and begin to operate differently. It means we are going to have to stop comparing the two worlds. We are going to have stop judging this one and instead celebrate it for all its wonderful creations. It's your own creations as much as everyone else's that are overwhelming you. When you acknowledge that fact, you feel less victimized. You wanted abundance and now you have it!

The good news is that once the majority of us are firmly planted in today's world, either through choice or attrition, I believe much of the stress will lift. This is because right now with two feet in opposite worlds, we are still trying to operate under the antiquated way of doing business and manifesting success. Under the old paradigm, the predominant belief system was that everything must be created through our own, individual sweat and tears. The masculine part of ourselves ruled, and therefore logic, direct action, competition, effort, and hard physical labor permeated our consciousness and directed our behavior. If we wanted to make it, we had to go after every single opportunity for fear that we might miss out on something and lose the chance of a lifetime.

Many of us are still caught up in that idea. We are therefore driving ourselves crazy, because instead of having a handful of customers to go visit, now there are potentially millions! Not only that, but all we have to do is to spend a few minutes online to notice there are many thousands of people with similar businesses trying to do the same thing we are, only with more resources at their disposal.

Now I know some of you are starting to sweat, but no worries! The fact of the matter is: if you've been reading this book, you don't have to worry about the competition. You've got the knowledge and tools you need to be successful if you choose to exercise them. It doesn't matter what everyone else is doing. There is an abundance of customers if you have the resources to deal with them. As we've discussed throughout this book, a large part of the solution is simply to disengage from the chaos around you by turning within, and calling upon your inner genie to do the work.

The people who can do this will thrive. The nations that can do this will be those that survive.

## There are always more
## options than you are aware of!

About five years ago when my first book was coming out, my publisher made it clear I needed to have
a website. I had known for a while that I needed a
website if I was ever going to leave my nine-to-five
job and work for myself. I had tried to hire someone
a few years back, but it was a disaster. He lost interest halfway through and shared neither my vision nor
my personal tastes in terms of color and design. Now I
needed a website fast and I didn't know where to turn.
I also didn't have extra money to spend. So I closed
my eyes, went inward, said some prayers, and visualized myself admiring my lovely, informative website.
That's when I saw an image of my ex-boyfriend Raul,
with whom I hadn't spoken in over a year.

Not surprisingly (well, not for me), the phone
rang about five minutes later. It was Raul. He told me
to check my e-mail because he was sending over a link
to his new website, which was only costing him a few
dollars per month. When I commented that I wished I
had his technological skills, he advised me that I didn't
need them, that websites now could be built with pre-
designed templates that might take the average person
an hour or two to become familiar with. The one he
was using was only costing him a few dollars a month.
Within a week my own site was up and running.

Today I have five websites hosted by three different companies, all of which I have built myself. It costs me less than three hundred dollars per year for all of them. (Of course five is too many! Now I'm working on consolidating them.) The best part of it all is that they are so easy and fun to build. Once I got over the learning curve, it wasn't much harder than learning how to use a basic word-processing program. In fact, I recently discovered that there are brand-new companies that offer website builder tools that are faster and more attractive than the ones I found just a couple of years ago. They make your site look like a scene from a major motion picture, with you as producer, director, editor, and star! The ease and beauty of these tools at my fingertips are so exciting that at times while working with them I've experienced what I can only describe as euphoria. Yes, I am a geek! But the point here is that what once seemed like a stressful burden has become one of my most fun pastimes.

There is never a reason why we can't accomplish or have something we need; it's just a matter of allowing our creative powers and intuition to open our minds to whole new approaches about which we were not previously aware. The avenues available to us for our creative expression and income flow are expanding along with the technology.

So, if you are a salesperson, ask yourself what else you can sell.

If you are a teacher, ask yourself what else you can teach.

If you are a teacher, ask yourself what you can sell.

If you are a salesperson, ask yourself what you can teach!

### When dreams collide

The most exciting thing for me about the entire alchemic/creative process is that it involves a merging of dreams. When we are fulfilling our own dreams, we are almost always doing so for someone else, too. There is never a lack of opportunity for this merging to occur, since so much of what we label *opportunity* is linked to other people who need us as much as we need them.

A little over a year ago I really began focusing on my desire to lose weight and get in shape. None of my clothes were fitting well, and I wasn't enjoying the extra jelly rolls around my waist, although they did seem to provide an endless source of amusement for the "boys" in my household. Since countless half-hearted attempts at dieting and exercising, either on my own or at gyms (which I disliked), had failed, I felt I really needed a personal trainer but didn't think I could afford one at the normal rates. Finally, I realized I had failed to elicit help from my inner genie in this area of my life. No wonder I was feeling stuck! I did the God as a magic symbol exercise in chapter 13. The results came in almost immediately.

At that time my son had already been taking classes at a martial-arts studio for about six months and was doing their after-school program. When I picked him up in the afternoons, I would see a group of women working out. I started to think I should look into these classes, but they were being taught by a man with whom I didn't feel much of a connection. Still, one day I talked to him, and he advised me that he was going to be leaving but that his partner, Cindy Blackwell, would be taking over. I could take as many as five classes per week with her and pay only about eighty dollars per month. It turned out Cindy was a personal trainer who had managed a major gym for several years. She had recently decided to begin teaching classes in addition to seeing private clients. The typical class size was two to five other students (mostly middle-aged moms like myself), and the classes were completely designed around our personal needs. I had manifested a personal trainer for only a few dollars an hour, at a place that I already had to be several days a week anyway!

### Cindy's story

Meanwhile, Cindy was working very hard. When her partner left the studio, she had to take out a loan so she could purchase all his equipment from him. Now she was paying several hundred dollars per month to teach classes out of the studio. Even though I was grateful for her low prices, I worried she wasn't getting paid what she was worth. She didn't have extra money for advertising and didn't really have the skills to market herself well. However, she continued for a year to show up to class, often twice a day. Even when she knew there would be only one student, she worked her hardest to get that student into shape.

While we, Cindy's students, were obviously becoming firmer, stronger, and healthier, we weren't meeting our weight-loss goals. She often discussed nutrition, but we weren't adjusting our diets on our own and she found this as frustrating as we did. However, that all changed one day because of a new idea that came to her. The idea was that she needed to take control of her students' diets; she decided she would begin to offer a program in which she would meet with each student once a week, and help them to prepare all their food for the week. The food would be placed in individual containers so every meal would be available when needed—in the correct portion size, with the correct number of calories and the correct fat and carbohydrate count. The meals would also be selected and prepared to satisfy individual tastes. Students could choose to prepare meals just for themselves or for their entire families. This process would take Cindy anywhere from three to four hours, and she would charge one hundred dollars for this food preparation. Since she was not just doing the cooking but also teaching, her students would soon be able to do the prep work themselves and therefore would no longer have to pay her, except for an occasional refresher session.

Within a week Cindy had her first student on board, and this student lost over twelve pounds in the first month. Her weight loss was so obvious that within two months Cindy had seven other students on board. With no advertising, she tripled her income. So far I have lost twenty-four pounds, and now I'm looking, eating, and feeling better than I have in years. For a while there, I used to think I was destined to become just a dumpy old housewife! Before I met Cindy I even bought a couple of the same kind of muumuus my grandmother used to wear! (Hello! This story is for all you middle-aged women—and men—out there who have decided that after a certain age, life just goes downhill; that's not reality, it's a *big, fat delusional lie!*)

I don't have even a particle of doubt that I will meet my final weight goal within two months, and I'm ready to meet the world. Cindy is well on her way to running a lucrative business. The moral of the story: All of this was accomplished by the converging of simple ideas and the will to carry them out. All of it happened without anyone having to pay for advertising or more than they could afford.

Isn't this colliding and merging of dreams really what our capitalistic society was built on? Yet somewhere along the way the dream part got distorted. Instead, some guy somewhere (probably a scrawny guy with glasses and a pocket protractor whose dad was a CEO of a company that he loved more than his son—no offense if that describes you!) realized that he might be able to make some extra bucks if he was able to manufacture our dreams for us, and that he'd be able to make even more money if he convinced us he was the only one who could deliver them.

## The future

Many people come to me and to psychics in general because they think they want or need to know what the future holds. I tell them it's not the future they are worried about; it's the feeling of stress that is running through their body right now that they are trying to find a way to deal with. When we deal with that first, and see what changes we can make in our life right now to create the future we desire, the urgency to know about the future diminishes, if not entirely disappears. (Of course it's always fun to take a peek anyway!) The solution is not to run and rerun this anxiety through your mind, but rather to release it and go do something that you enjoy, that makes you feel good about yourself and the world. This is what I suggest for you now.

There are many folks—scientists, inventors, and artists—creating wonderful things and doing everything possible to improve and save us and the world we live in. Either become one of these innovators or discover how to support one or more of them. If you can't make a financial contribution, then take such people out to dinner or volunteer to baby-sit their kids.

I believe the Catholic church had it right when it requested that its parishioners tithe a percentage of their income. The problem was that much of the money went into buildings instead of people. There is so much we can do for each other. Taxation is a form of tithing, but the problem is that we really don't have a say in whether we want to contribute financially or what is done with our tax dollars. Can you imagine what a difference it would make if we could actually choose which programs our tax dollars were going to fund? This might sound silly, but it wouldn't be that hard to pull off if we were given a checklist at the time we filed. Could you imagine the difference it would make in our willingness to pay and our attitudes about taxes in general? We would then be a lot closer to having the democracy we've been told we have. This would also ensure that people paid much closer attention to what their government is doing and offering to its people. The people would become part of the government, as was perhaps the original plan.

The economic catastrophe of the present time has brought about
a condition of mass terror, and the more sensitive the individual,
the more he will react to this state of mind. Fear of the future is
therefore a distressing blend of instinctual memory and anticipatory
imagination, and few there are who escape this menace. Worry and
anxiety are the lot of every man and cannot and will not be offset
and overcome by any lesser factor than the soul itself.
—ALICE BAILEY, 1934

# 18

# HOW TO CHANGE
# THE WORLD

## The week the world changed forever

There it was. The book was complete. Tomorrow I
would e-mail it to my editor and go back to having
a life. I went to bed with mixed feelings. Yes, I had
crawled out of my black hole into a sunny optimism
that glimmered seductively from the final pages of my
manuscript. And yet, what had really changed? I mean,
had shifting my inner reality during the past nine
months really had an impact on the world around me?

The next day I looked around my house. Well, it looked a little cleaner. The guys had finally figured out if they wanted the dishes done or the garbage taken out in the final days leading up to my deadline, they were going to have to do it themselves. Danny had even started bringing me my cups of coffee instead of complaining about the stains they were making on the brand-new counter tops of our lovely new house. Oh yes, I almost forgot: this house was a change! When I first began this chapter, the three of us were living in a tiny one-bedroom guest house and were ready to kill each other. Now we were living in a gorgeous, fully restored 1920s home that was six times the size of our last place, close enough to my son's school that he could walk there, and that gave me my own private office in which to write.

I next walked into the bathroom, not really sure what kind of change I might find there, when I tripped over the scale. Okay, well, I have lost twenty-four pounds. That was a change.

Then I stepped outside to my driveway, where my 1992 Oldsmobile with a broken air conditioner and smashed-in trunk had been. In its place was a 2001 Mercedes-Benz with only a couple of little dings in it. Okay, that was a change. I strolled through the garden we'd planted just the month before, and noticed the flowers were filling the garden and spreading out nicely, as were the weeds.

Okay, so my personal life has changed, but what about the outside world? I realized if I was going to find any changes with the world, I'd need to be able to see farther than my driveway or halfway down the street (even if my street looks like much of the rest of the world, since we live in a neighborhood filled mostly with immigrants, both legal and illegal). So, in order to check out the state of the world, I did what any normal American would do. I went back inside my house, closed the blinds, and turned on the news.

And that's when I discovered that the American financial empire had fallen.

Nope, not done yet!

In an article in the September 26, 2008, edition of the *New York Times*, Eric Dash and Andrew Ross Sorkin summed up the course of events that led to the toppling of the financial empire in the second half of that year:

> *Washington Mutual, the giant lender that came to symbolize the excesses of the mortgage boom, was seized by federal regulators on Thursday night, in what is by far the largest bank failure in American history . . . The government has dealt with troubled financial institutions differently. Lehman Brothers and Washington Mutual, which were less entangled with the rest of the financial system, were allowed to collapse. But the government took*

*emergency measures to stabilize Goldman Sachs,*
*Morgan Stanley, and the American International*
*Group, the insurance giant . . . [Washington*
*Mutual] offered complex mortgages and credit*
*cards whose terms made it easy for the least cred-*
*itworthy borrowers to get financing, a strategy the*
*bank extended in big cities . . . But underneath the*
*hood, the bank's machinery was failing. Then the*
*housing market began to crumble . . .*

### Awareness is the doorway to progress

These "emergency measures" to stabilize the banking industry included Congress handing over seven hundred billion dollars of taxpayer money to the executives of these failing banks, the very executives who had mismanaged, gambled, and extorted the people's money in the first place. Most Americans I speak to are outraged, as they don't see this as a long-term solution. I don't either, but I understand it.

This fear-based reaction to the crumbling of a flawed system is no different from how we as individuals react when something in our lives falls apart. We scramble to put back the pieces as quickly as possible, hoping we can just continue on with business as usual. In the same way, governments and societies need time to adjust. It's okay that our leaders cannot yet see an alternative way of doing business. They will. Some of them are really smart. We tend to think there is no time, but actually, what's the hurry? We will be okay, because we have our inner genies working for us.

While I know many people are enduring financial hardships, and I do very much feel for them, at the same time I am optimistic. I know in my heart that for us as a people and as a nation, this is a step in the right direction. I know that those who have or will be losing their homes or savings will be able to replace them, whether with new material goods or qualities within themselves that emerge as a result of lessons learned during this crisis. Some of the people who have lost their homes were actually in extreme distress for quite a while leading up to the loss, because they had gotten themselves in far too deep and were not seeing their way out. Others have sacrificed their soul for years in jobs they hated, and while this makes it seem even more cruel that they would lose even a single hard-earned cent, there are lessons here as well— one of which is that the security most of us seek is not to be found in a paycheck or a retirement account, but rather somewhere within.

This is not just a financial crisis; it is a spiritual one as well. I am therefore relieved, because there really is always light at the end of the tunnel if you are willing to continue on that far. A cumbersome weight has been lifted from my heart, as my wish for awareness of the underlying greed and flaws of our current economic system has just been granted. I know for some this feels like the end of the world, but actually it's the end of economic enslavement. The beginning of a new way of being has not yet emerged on a global scale, but I believe the seeds of change have begun to sprout under the fertile soil of humanity's desire for change. This was symbolized by the election in 2008 of Barack Obama, a man whose presidency was made possible by the vision, courage, and efforts of those who were able to remain larger than the crisis and pain they were in, not so long ago.

**Don't underestimate the power of your attention**
When you put your mind on anything, you experience more of that thing. In the work I do, this means that as soon as people put a majority of their attention on their own psychic abilities, they begin to have psychic experiences. When they put their attention on out-of-body travel, they begin to have out-of-body experiences. As soon as they put their attention on synchronicity, synchronistic events happen. As soon as they put their attention on love, their hearts begin to open. The more physical action they take in alignment with these goals, the faster things start to occur. This is true regardless of whether or not they have ever heard of the law of attraction.

I have some friends who are involved in spirit photography. Everything from colorful orbs to brilliantly colored lights to detailed human faces appear in their photos. The more attention they give to these photos, the more these phenomena show up. The less attention they give to them, the less they appear. When I teach a class, whatever we set as a group intention seems to happen.

**The power of the group**

Creating as a group can be extremely powerful! This is why if you have the opportunity to study anything, particularly pertaining to spirit, you quite often will achieve more within a group setting than by working individually, although the results may not be apparent until you return home and spend some time alone, where you can assimilate and integrate the shifts you made during the group experience. You can think of each person as a pot of energy. When you pour the contents of all the pots together, you have one giant cauldron or swimming pool! When the energy is consolidated and directed, this bastion of energy creates a force that has the power to cut through the preexisting reality that denies the power of spirit.

When people come together, they can therefore part the sea of limitations long enough for miracles to occur. When the members of any group are aware of the power they possess as individuals and as a group, they become even more powerful. Eventually, some of the individuals raise their own awareness and energy field enough so that they adopt a new overriding reality, and now can achieve as individuals what was only previously possible with the group or with the tutelage of a spiritual teacher, such as a guru. Many people, however, get stuck believing it was the group or the teacher who possesses the power. That is when they lose themselves.

### How is it that we are content to crawl?

In 1894 Baird T. Spalding embarked on an expedition with ten other researchers. In *Life and Teaching of the Masters of the Far East*, Spalding recounts his observations of numerous "masters" in India and Tibet, who were often able to perform seemingly impossible tasks, such as instantly manifesting enough food out of thin air to sustain their entire group for weeks at a time. These experiences forced Spalding to reexamine every notion he had held to be true.

The following account, from Spalding's *Life and Teaching of the Masters of the Far East*, first published in 1924, takes place during a long journey on foot, on a day when these researchers—guided by three men with extraordinary powers named Jast, Emil, and Neprow—were joined by four strangers who wished to reach a village located on the opposite side of a raging river:

> *The afternoon of our third day out, we came to the bank of a larger river. The stream was about two thousand feet wide, running bank-full, and*

*the current was at least ten miles per hour . . . We were informed that we would be able to cross by bridge farther up stream, but to reach this bridge would necessitate a detour of at least four days' hard travel . . . It had been demonstrated to us that we need not take any thought as to our provisions for, from the day already referred to, when our provisions were exhausted, the whole company, consisting of over three hundred persons, had been supplied with an abundance of provisions from the invisible, as we called it. This supply was maintained for sixty-four days . . .*

Spalding continues with an even more remarkable account:

*. . . We thought it rather foolhardy to attempt to swim a stream as swift as the one before us just to make a friendly call upon a neighbor. We felt that swimming was the only way the crossing could be accomplished. When Jast rejoined the group, the twelve, fully dressed, walked to the bank of the stream, and with the utmost composure stepped on the water, not into it. I never shall forget my feelings as I saw each of those twelve men step from solid ground upon the running water. I held my breath, expecting, of course, to see them plunge beneath and disappear . . . I think each of us held his breath, until they were all past midstream, so*

*astonished were we to see these twelve men walk-*
*ing calmly across the surface of the stream . . .*
*and not sinking below the soles of their sandals.*

Spalding explains that Jast and Neprow told him and the other researchers that the researchers could also cross the river and be safe, but they just could not believe this, so they opted instead to take the four-day detour around the river by land. A leader of the group later spoke to the researchers as they toiled up the side of a mountain, asking:

"How is it, if a few are able to do the things we have seen accomplished, that all men cannot accomplish the same things? How is it that man is content to crawl, and not only content to crawl but is obliged to do so?"

Then the other leader, Jast, who had already demonstrated his ability to materialize and dematerialize his body at will and be in two places at once, spoke up:

*Do you think that the men you saw walk across the stream yesterday to save themselves the incon-venience of this trip are in any way special cre-ations any more than you are? No. They are not created in any way different from you. They do not have one atom more power than you were created with. They have, by the right use of their thought forces, developed their God-given power. The things you have seen accomplished while you have been with us, you, yourselves, can accom-*

*plish just as fully and freely. The things you have*
*seen are accomplished in accord with definite law*
*and every human being can use the law if he will.*

## Modern-day masters

In August 2007 the World Council of Elders held the
first International Sundance in Montana. This was the
first time that native elders representing very different
tribes from the four corners of the globe agreed to put
aside their differences and join together in prayer and
dance for the sake of healing the earth and all of its
people. The timing was not a coincidence, but rather
the fulfillment of an ancient prophecy shared by several tribes. One hundred and twenty-five participants
gathered from cultures and places as diverse as Australia, India, Japan, Siberia, Guatemala, Hawaii, and
Canada to participate in the most sacred ceremony of
the first peoples of the northern Great Plains, the Sundance. Michael Tamura, author of *You Are the Answer*,
was invited to participate in the ceremony as a dancer
representing the east. During a recent seminar and in
a subsequent conversation, Michael provided a fascinating account of the events that transpired over the
course of eight days.

Michael explained how he and a few others worked
tirelessly around the clock for four days to prepare the
sacred arbor in which the ceremony would take place.
This involved clearing the ground of all foliage and

rocks, and uprooting a very large tree and carrying it by hand to the center of the arbor, where it was transplanted and decorated with hundreds of colorful prayer ties and flags that took each dancer a full day to make.

This process was followed by four days and nights of praying and dancing, while fasting from all food and abstaining from water. On the final day, Michael, a fifty-four-year-old slender healer who had almost died from a heart attack less than six months earlier, allowed the medicine man to pierce his chest four times with a knife, making cuts in his flesh that formed flaps through which three-inch wooden dowels were inserted. Ropes were then inserted into the hollow dowels and tied together, forming a single rope, the end of which was connected to a log and strung over the branch of the tree to secure it in place. Michael was then instructed to move farther away from the tree, causing the rope to grow taut and pulling the skin away from his chest.

Michael recounted that except for when his chest was being cut, he continued to dance around the tree for several minutes. Finally, he was instructed to move backward and place his hands on the back of his hips. Two of his students, one a medical doctor, then slipped a log through the space between his arms and his back and moved him backward until the dowels broke through his flesh, releasing him.

Michael explained that initially he wasn't going to participate in this part of the ceremony; however, at one point during the day he received the message from spirit that this was exactly what he needed to do. He recalled how right before the incisions were made, Jesus appeared next to him, laughing, and asked him, "Does this remind you of anything?"

Michael was then shown pictures of the past life he had with Jesus, in which he had felt guilty for not being able to save him. Then Jesus told him, "Now you are going to experience exactly what I went through on the cross."

Michael suddenly understood that, contrary to popular thought, Jesus had not suffered on that cross at all, and Michael knew that he would therefore not suffer through the piercing of the Sundance. So he began praying as hard as he could, commanding his spirit into God's hands while imploring that those who would cause him pain be forgiven.

Apparently, Jesus was right! Michael swears he never felt any pain. Even when his flesh broke from the increasing tension on the rope, he recalls hearing a snap and seeing a flash of light like an explosion. Instead of pain, he felt only bliss.

Michael firmly believes that "life doesn't demand that you have to suffer, it's people who do." He also distinguishes between "overcoming suffering" and "choosing not to suffer at all." He explained that he decided to go ahead with the piercing because he realized that it was an opportunity to demonstrate this truth to others, even his loved ones, who apparently suffered tremendously as they stood by, helpless, watching him *not* suffering! (Of course, at the time no one knew what Michael was going through, or if his heart was strong enough to endure what to outsiders looked like torture.)

I believe that, among other reasons, rituals such as the Sundance are so powerful because of the intensive preparation involved. This preparation leads to a tremendous harnessing of human energy. When many people come together with a single purpose or shared prayer, this energy becomes a torpedo that cannot be intercepted. Through the intensive power of prayer, devotion, faith, and love, the dancers, surrounded by a hundred supporters outside the circle, actually created a force field in which the law of spirit reigned over the perceived limitations of the physical world.

As Michael explained, the moment he crossed into the arbor, it was as if he were inside a different universe, where the other dancers no longer looked like people but instead like blazing dancers of light. He told me, "In this sacred space, pain does not exist and thus it is not experienced. Pain is the perception of one's sense of separateness." While I haven't witnessed this myself, I've seen dozens of photographs of ceremonies in which the participants looked as if they were in various stages of disappearing—with one part of their body appearing solid, the other part as light.

### Psychic surgery: the "bloody operation"

When I lived in the Philippines in 1997 and 1998, I was studying with a healer named Brother William, who performed what the people called the "bloody operation." His "clinic" was a ramshackle structure with only half a tin roof, set way down in a canyon on the outskirts of the city of Baguio, beneath a police checkpoint. To get to it you had to stumble down a very steep and often muddy path. What was almost as intriguing to me as the healing taking place was the fact that every morning I'd arrive at eight o'clock and find no less than a hundred people already seated on wooden benches. I was never sure how some of them—people who were quite frail, sick, and old—made it down there when I could barely do it without sliding down on my butt.

Brother William usually healed his patients by placing his hands on an afflicted part of the client's body. The body of a patient would seemingly open up under his hands. He'd then extract matter that resembled blood and tissue, which he felt was the physical manifestation of the disease. Morning after morning I stood only inches from his table, watching him work with hundreds of people in this manner.

One morning he instructed me to take a pair of tweezers down from the wall and bring it over to the patient lying on the bare wooden table before him. He placed his hands on her chest and opened it up. He muttered, "Cancer." He then reached inside, squeezing the skin a bit, revealing a tumor. Next, he gestured for me to pull the tumor out with the tweezers.

I gasped, but Brother William merely gestured at me to proceed. After another moment's hesitation, I went for it. I was surprised to discover that the tumor was connected to other tissue from which I had to detach it. The moment the tumor was removed, Brother William took his hands away and the woman's chest closed up. There was no visible scar.

Sometimes I start to question whether or not this all really happened. What I can say with certainty is that I did reach into this woman's open chest and pull out this tumor, and I watched her chest close back up while dozens of observers stood peering over my shoulder.

### In conclusion

"What's going to change the world is not activism,
but the increasing frequency of love."
—RICHARD BARTLETT, CREATOR OF MATRIX ENERGETICS

I present these experiences because they remind us, they remind me, that anything is possible. If we can overcome pain and perform surgery with our bare hands, if people can walk on water or manifest an abundance of food where there wasn't any before, then are any of our own problems, any of the world's problems, truly too difficult to solve or reverse? For that matter, are there even such things as problems, or are these merely illusions or lessons that we incorrectly define as "problems"?

What do you think life would be like if we came together as millions of people from across the globe, and consciously agreed to raise our energy so that the pain of the masses was transformed into global bliss? What if we all decided that no matter what is happening around us, suffering isn't truly necessary? What if we raised the havingness of all human beings, so that we not only expected, but demanded, that every man, woman, and child be given the opportunity to live in a beautiful and comfortable house, get the absolute best education, have the best health care, and enjoy the riches previously relegated to kings, presidents, and congressmen?

I presented this question recently to a friend, who insisted this was impossible. He said there were too many people with too many children, and therefore there was no way everyone could live like royalty. I disagree. In Amish communities, every man is assured a house because it's expected that the members of the community will help him build the house as if it were their own. There is no reason why this practice can't be carried out within the rest of American society. It's only when we buy into the idea of rugged individualism, that it's every person for himself or herself, or even every family for themselves, that there are the "haves" and the "have-nots." Then of course there is the predominant and problematic belief that there need even *be* haves and have-nots, not to mention the belief structures held by many of the "have-nots," belief structures that persist in telling them that they cannot have what they desire.

Obviously, the socioeconomic-political-legal structure we have in America and elsewhere is not working well for the majority of citizens anymore. I believe we are witnessing the fall of this outdated system, but we cannot yet get a clear sense of what will replace it. This new system will become clearer as mass numbers of people begin to shift their energetic frequencies and their consciousness, which involves the expansion of their heart energy. These things are not linear. Each one impacts the other, just as every person impacts every other person. When one thought is shifted, the energetic frequency shifts, and the heart can open. When the heart opens, all else shifts. When emotions, which are strong frequencies, change (through meditation, through exchanges of love and forgiveness, or by engaging with others who are already vibrating differently, in person or through their writings), we begin to love ourselves, love others, release fears, and then become capable of what are now considered miracles, but what will someday soon (I believe) become the status quo.

This process explains why so many effective and different healing modalities are out there. They all lead to a similar result—the evolution of humanity—although I do believe that certain modalities—many of which are offered in this book, in my other two books, and those books not yet written—can work much faster than others!

This transformational process has been happening for years now, and it coincides with the technological revolution and our current economic and energy crises (which could also be defined as a global growth period or a dark night of the soul). In the same way that technology has exponentially expanded in recent years, so has the spiritual evolution of humanity. This fact will be quite clear to some of you, while to others it may not yet make sense at all. Suffice it to say that the changes in our political and economic systems will correspond with a change in our personal and global energetic systems. Along with this change, or even to speed it along, it will help if we as a people, whether the people of the United States or the people of the world, come together with a unified vision. As evidenced by the election of Barack Obama to the presidency (let's not forget that he wrote a book so aptly entitled *The Audacity of Hope*), I believe that we are ready to do this. So then the question is: how do we get the people together in a unified vision?

Last year, ninety-seven million votes came in to select the winner of *American Idol*, and more people watched the season finale of that show than tuned in to most political programming. I believe TV shows like *American Idol*, which admittedly may be cheesy, do reflect the creativity and dreams of so many. If we could harness the enthusiasm and interest that people have for cultural phenomena like *American Idol*, and use that energy for more important purposes—to bring us together—just think of what we could accomplish!

Imagine if the president called an emergency press conference in which he or she requested the presence of every American citizen. With very little time or effort, every major network would broadcast this message to tens of millions of Americans. The president could then lead everyone in prayers and visualizations concerning any number of topics. Imagine if instead of our leaders standing up and saying, "We must kill the Muslim terrorists who wish to destroy us," the president said, "We are going to try something new. Before we resort to other measures, we are going to try an experiment. I want every American to turn inward, and visualize all Muslims standing together, filled with light, living abundant and joyful lives. See them living heaven on earth. Imagine that they are hugging you, and you are hugging them back and laughing and crying together." Ironically, a simple move such as this would actually take more courage from a president than a declaration of war.

Now some Americans will say, "That would never work; they hate us too much." But let me ask you, if redirecting energy through intentional thought can heal the pain between individuals in the same country, then why can't it heal the pain between citizens of different countries? Or even between people and the earth? Why haven't we given this a try in America?

Imagine if all along, all these years, it turned out that all the wars, the laws, the fighting, the suing, the blaming, the drilling, and the suffering had been unnecessary. Imagine if all we needed to do was get enough people together and make a single, united wish. Wouldn't we feel just a little bit silly for all the time and energy we had wasted? I believe we would. However, I'm willing to take that risk.

How about you?

# BiBLIOGRAPHY

Blavatsky, H. P. (Helena Petrovna). *The Secret Doctrine.* Wheaton, IL: Quest Books, 1993.

Bloom, Howard. *Global Brain: The Evolution of Mass Mind from the Big Bang to the 21st Century.* New York: Wiley, 2000.

———. *Reinventing Capitalism: Putting Soul in the Machine.* (Unpublished material.) See http://www .howardbloom.net/reinventing_capitalism/ (accessed 4 February 2009).

Byrne, Rhonda. *The Secret*. New York: Atria Books/ Beyond Words, 2006.

Calaprice, Alice, ed. *The New Quotable Einstein*. Princeton, NJ: Princeton University Press, 2005.

Cayce, Edgar. *The Lost Memoirs of Edgar Cayce*. Virginia Beach, VA: A. R. E. Press, 1997.

Choquette, Sonia. *Your Heart's Desire: Instructions for Creating the Life You Really Want*. New York: Three Rivers Press, 1997.

Dash, Eric, and Andrew Ross Sorkin. "Government Seizes WaMu and Sells Some Assets." *New York Times*, September 26, 2008, p. A1.

Dyer, Wayne. *You'll See It When You Believe It: The Way to Your Personal Transformation*. New York: Harper Paperbacks, 2001.

Gawain, Shakti. *Living in the Light: A Guide to Personal and Planetary Transformation*. Novato, CA: New World Library, 1998.

Gilbert, Elizabeth. *Eat, Pray, Love: One Woman's Search for Everything Across Italy, India and Indonesia*. New York: Penguin, 2007.

Hicks, Esther, Jerry Hicks, and Abraham (spirit). *Ask and It Is Given: Learning to Manifest Your Desires*. Carlsbad, CA: Hay House, 2004.

Icke, David . . . *And the Truth Shall Set You Free*. Ryde, UK: David Icke Books, 2004.

Katz, Debra Lynne. *You Are Psychic: The Art of Clairvoyant Reading & Healing.* St. Paul, MN: Llewellyn, 2004.

———. *Extraordinary Psychic: Proven Techniques to Master Your Natural Psychic Abilities.* Woodbury, MN: Llewellyn, 2008.

Klein, Alec. "Credit Raters' Power Leads to Abuses, Some Borrowers Say." *Washington Post,* November 24, 2004, p. A1.

McTaggart, Lynne. *The Intention Experiment: Using Your Thoughts to Change Your Life and the World.* New York: Free Press, 2008.

Monroe, Robert A. *Journeys Out of the Body.* New York: Doubleday, 1991.

Murphy, Joseph. *The Power of Your Subconscious Mind.* Revised and expanded edition. Paramus, NJ: Reward Books, 2000.

Radin, Dean. *The Conscious Universe: The Scientific Truth of Psychic Phenomena.* New York: HarperEdge, 1997.

———. *Entangled Minds: Extrasensory Experiences in a Quantum Reality.* New York: Paraview Pocket Books, 2006.

Roberts, Jane, and Seth (spirit). *The Nature of Personal Reality: Specific, Practical Techniques for Solving Everyday Problems and Enriching the Life You Know.* San Rafael, CA: New World Library, 1994.

———. *Seth Speaks: The Eternal Validity of the Soul.* San Rafael, CA: New World Library, 1994.

Roman, Sanaya, and Duane Packer. *Creating Money: Attracting Abundance*, second edition. Tiburon, CA: H J Kramer/New World Library, 2008.

Shinn, Florence Scovel. *The Wisdom of Florence Scovel Shinn*. New York: Simon & Schuster, 1989.

Spalding, Baird T. *Life and Teaching of the Masters of the Far East* (volumes 1 and 2). Marina del Rey, CA: DeVorss, 1978.

Strelkoff, Lyena. *Caterpillar Soup*, a one-woman-show script (unpublished).

Tamura, Michael J. *You Are the Answer: Discovering and Fulfilling Your Soul's Purpose*. Woodbury, MN: Llewellyn, 2007.

Toffler, Alvin. *The Third Wave*. New York: Bantam/William Morrow, 1980.

Tolle, Eckhart. *A New Earth: Awakening to Your Life's Purpose*. New York: Dutton, 2005.

————. *The Power of Now: A Guide to Spiritual Enlightenment*. Novato, CA: New World Library, 2004.

Walker, Alice. *Possessing the Secret of Joy*. New York: Washington Square Press, 1997.

Walsch, Neale Donald. *Conversations with God: An Uncommon Dialogue*. New York: Putnam, 1996.

Woolf, Virginia. *A Room of One's Own*. New York: Harcourt, 1991.

Zinn, Howard. *A People's History of the United States*. New edition. New York: Harper Collins, 2003.

# GLOSSARY

AFFIRMATION: A statement that declares an intention or condition for a desirable outcome. Affirmations are used on a conscious level to reprogram subconscious or limited beliefs.

ASTRAL PROJECTION OR ASTRAL TRAVEL: The ability of one's spirit to leave the body and travel on the astral plane or in other dimensions. This is also referred to as an "out-of-body experience." It can be done with or without awareness, and to various degrees. It can occur spontaneously through intention.

ATHEISM:  A lack of belief in the spiritual, including God, psychic phenomena, or the human soul.

AURA:  The energetic field surrounding every living organism, which contains information about the organism and energies affecting it. The aura can be thought of as the organism's spirit that extends outward from the body.

AWARENESS:  Having knowledge through focused attention.

CATERPILLAR SOUP:  A term created by Lyena Strelkoff that describes the uneasy period a person goes through in the process of transformation, when they have changed from one state of being but have not yet reached a state that allows them to form a new definition of themselves. This is also referred to as an *intensive growth period* and can lead to what mystics refer to as the *dark night of the soul*.

CHAKRAS:  Sanskrit word for "spinning wheels," chakras are energy centers that correspond to specific parts of the human body and that regulate the body's overall functioning.

CHANNELING: A psychic ability in which a person receives and communicates information coming directly from a source outside themselves.

CLAIRAUDIENCE: A psychic ability in which information inaudible to human ears is heard inside one's mind.

CLAIRSENTIENCE: A psychic ability in which information is received through touch or on a physical body level.

CLAIRVOYANCE: A psychic ability located within one's third eye, or sixth chakra, that involves accessing information in the form of visions, images, and pictures.

CLAIRVOYANT HEALING: An act in which visualization is utilized to eliminate or transmute emotional or physical pain or negative energies, and restore one to a healthier state.

CLAIRVOYANT READING: An act in which information in the form of mental images, visions, and pictures is accessed.

CONSCIOUS CREATION: Creating one's own existence with purpose and awareness, and by harnessing the power of one's mind and feeling.

CONTROL FREAK: A person who needs to understand or determine every element in life and interferes with the natural course of things, or who expends energy trying to control that which is out of his or her control. A control freak is one who attempts to circumvent another's will through the control freak's own interpretation of it.

COSMIC ENERGY:   Energy that originates from the air, sun, atmosphere, the spiritual realm, or God.

CREATING/CREATION:   To bring into being.

CREATIVE ENERGY:   An energy that begins in the reproductive area of the body that can create any project. The more this energy is running, the more free we are to come up with new ideas and ways of being, and the more passion for life we have.

EARTH ENERGY:   Energy that originates from within the earth. It is naturally running through each of our bodies all the time, assisting us with our connection to the planet and our body.

ENERGY:   Life force; the essence of all things physical and nonphysical. Matter, spirit, atoms, thoughts, emotions, and pain are all energy.

ENLIGHTENMENT:   A state in which a person has become actualized, has accumulated a certain level of wisdom; when a person's body, mind, and spirit are fully integrated and the person's being holds more lightness than darkness.

EXCUSE: A justification that is either untrue or disguises one's true feelings or thoughts in order to deflect responsibility from oneself.

EXPECTATION: A predetermined set of ideas of how an event will unfold or how another person or oneself should behave.

EXTRASENSORY PERCEPTION: Perceiving information through means other than the five physical senses.

FEMININE OR FEMALE ENERGY: A polarized energy that is receptive, passive, open, and intuitive. It is guided, shaped, or manipulated by the masculine aspect.

GENIE WITHIN, THE: A term for the creative force within oneself that can be activated, strengthened, and utilized in order to achieve one's goals and manifest one's dreams.

GROUNDING CORD: An energetic connection securing an object or a person to the earth. Foreign energies can be released through this cord through conscious intent and visualization.

GROWTH PERIOD: An intense period of personal transformation during which one's beliefs, thoughts, perceptions, and self-image are altered. This can result in a temporary period of emotional or cognitive turbulence.

HAVINGNESS: The extent to which a person can allow himself or herself to have abundance.

IMAGINATION: The act or power of creating images or ideas in the mind.

INTENTION: Focus with a desired outcome.

INTUITION: The act of listening and responding to one's feelings or thoughts, the cause of which cannot easily be explained by logical processes. This is a word that is often used in place of the term *psychic ability*, because intuition describes a common experience among the mainstream population and is therefore generally found more acceptable by those who have a resistance to the term *psychic ability*, even though they essentially mean the same thing.

KNOWINGNESS: A psychic ability located in the seventh, or crown, chakra, in which a person instantaneously knows information in the form of a thought, without having to go through logical steps to gain that information.

LAW: A set of rules that describes but does not explain an occurrence in nature.

LAW OF ATTRACTION: The force, or invisible power, by which a body (your body) draws anything to itself while resisting separation from that same thing. This force is created through manipulation of one's own thoughts and emotions.

LIBRARY OF SYMBOLS: A collection of symbolic images, utilized by those who work with clairvoyance or visualization in order to interpret clairvoyant information.

LIMIT: The point at which a person is limited within his or her imagination. The threshold of what a person allows himself or herself to have, which is dictated by the person's belief system and feelings of deservedness. The point at which a person feels he or she can or should not go any further in allowing himself or herself to experience something. Limits can easily be surpassed once the person becomes aware of the limits or has an experience that is outside the range of the limit.

MANIFESTATION: A form in which a being manifests itself or is thought to manifest itself, especially the material or bodily form of a spirit.

MANIFESTING: The creative act of transforming a thought into the material plane.

MARTYR COMPLEX: A self-defeating set of beliefs and behaviors that cause people to gain satisfaction and elevated self-esteem by sacrificing their own pleasure and needs for the sake of others.

MASCULINE OR MALE ENERGY:  A polarized energy or quality that is goal-driven and oriented toward action and physical activity. It is focused outside itself, and is controlling, domineering, and attempts to direct its feminine counterpart.

MASS CONSCIOUSNESS:  A phenomenon that occurs among groups of people, in which energies merge and people adopt each other's beliefs, thoughts, and emotions—sometimes at the expense of their individual beliefs and codes of ethics.

MATERIALIZE:  To appear suddenly, to bring a thought into being on the material level.

MEDITATION:  Turning attention inward to bring one's mind to a state of stillness, where subtler energies and information can be experienced.

NEUTRALITY:  Being neutral; maintaining a state of emotional and cognitive balance that is not invested in a particular outcome.

NONATTACHMENT:  Having no emotional investment in an object or an outcome of a situation.

OBSTACLE:  Something usually perceived to be standing in the way or inhibiting a goal or forward movement.

OMNIPRESENT: Being everywhere all at once.

OMNISCIENT: All knowing.

PRECOGNITION: Knowing that something is going to happen before it happens.

PROCLAMATION: A message that is declared with certainty and unwavering confidence.

PROGRAMMING: Beliefs, thoughts, ethics, information, feelings, or perceptions that are passed from one person to another and that may or may not be in harmony with the recipient's own spiritual goals, information, or way of being.

PROJECTION: Seeing one's own qualities in someone else, often unconsciously; assigning particular attributes to another that really belong to oneself.

PSYCHIC EXPERIENCE: A supernatural experience in which information is sent or received through means other than the five senses.

PSYCHIC TOOLS: Visualization techniques that affect and influence energy that can be utilized for psychic reading and healing and to enhance the qualities of one's life.

RESISTANCE: An energy or mental attitude that insists something should be other than it is. This attitude causes the one who holds it stress, anxiety, and negative thinking.

RUNNING ENERGY:   The act of visualizing the movement of energy, in the form of light, color, or water, through one's body, aura, or surroundings in order to facilitate the release of foreign or unhealthy energies and/or to replenish oneself with a higher vibrational frequency.

SELF-ENERGIZATION:   Calling one's life force to oneself.

SELF-ESTEEM:   The ability and extent to which a person cherishes oneself.

SKEPTICISM:   A closed state of mind in which one doubts or questions things, sometimes to the point where these doubts obscure the truth.

SOUL MATE:   A spirit with whom one has a deep affinity and connection, and with whom one reconnects throughout many incarnations. This spirit may currently be in the form of another person, an animal, or a nonphysical entity, and these forms may change from one incarnation to the next.

SPIRIT:   The essence of a person.

SPIRITUAL ALCHEMY:   Transforming one form of matter or one experience into another by utilizing one's full range of spiritual abilities. This also includes manifesting something that exists only on the mental or spiritual plane onto the physical plane.

SPIRITUAL PATH:   A course that one's spirit is destined to follow in order to gain certain life experiences while in the physical body.

SPIRITUALITY:   The act of acknowledging and paying attention to one's own spirit and the spirits of others.

SUBCONSCIOUS MIND:   Existing or operating in the mind beneath or beyond conscious awareness.

SUPERNATURAL:   Beyond the physical senses.

SYMBOL:   An object or sign that represents another object, idea, person, or quality.

THIRD EYE:   The center of one's clairvoyance. The third eye corresponds with the sixth chakra and is located behind the forehead, slightly above and between the physical eyes.

TRANSFORMATION:   To effect change. To move from one state of being to another, often denoting progress.

UNCONSCIOUS:   A lack of awareness of one's own mind or actions.

VALIDATION:   To confirm one's value.

VIBRATIONAL FREQUENCY:   The rate at which the atoms and subparticles of a being or object vibrate. The higher this frequency is, the closer it is to the frequency of light. It is within this frequency that the law of attraction can operate most efficiently. This state also facilitates a state of well-being.

Visualization:   The act of calling forth images, visions, and pictures into one's mind.